PLAYS TWO

Lope de Vega
PLAYS TWO

A BOND HONOURED
by John Osborne

Based on *La Fianza Satisfecha* by Lope de Vega

THE LABYRINTH OF DESIRE
by Lope de Vega

Translated by Michael Jacobs

La Prueba de los Ingenios

Introduction by Michael Jacobs

OBERON BOOKS
LONDON

A Bond Honoured first published in 1966 by Faber and Faber.

First published in this collection in 2002 by Oberon Books Ltd. (incorporating Absolute Classics)
521 Caledonian Road, London N7 9RH
Tel: 020 7607 3637 / Fax: 020 7607 3629
e-mail: oberon.books@btinternet.com
www.oberonbooks.com

A catalogue record for this book is available from the British Library.

ISBN: 1 84002 180 2

Cover design: Andrzej Klimowski

Printed in Great Britain by Antony Rowe Ltd, Chippenham.

Contents

Introduction

Michael Jacobs

Even a random dip into Lope de Vega's 350 or so surviving plays is likely to yield surprising rewards, with sometimes the most bizarre and apparently ludicrous works proving to have elements that strike a contemporary note. It is difficult to imagine what factor other than chance led someone in the 1960s to propose *A Bond Honoured*[1] to the then Literary Manager of Britain's National Theatre, Kenneth Tynan. Given the number of well-known works by Lope that are yet to be properly staged in Britain, not to mention his many outstanding plays awaiting rediscovery even in Spain itself, this was not the most obvious choice for adaptation. A tale of a monster (Leonido) who achieves redemption through Christ and crucifixion, *A Bond Honoured* is a religious work whose subject-matter can hardly be deemed sympathetic or fully comprehensible to a modern and non-Catholic audience. It is uneven in quality, and has only come down to us in a mutilated version that is missing many lines of verse. In the canon of Lope's plays established in 1968 by the scholars S Griswold Morley and Courtney Bruerton[2], it even ranks in the category of 'doubtful works'.

Tynan had a literal translation of the play sent to John Osborne, who does not appear to have had any especial love of Lope de Vega, nor any great knowledge of Spanish drama. Driven by the belief that the British 'have the greatest body of dramatic literature in the world' (a view he felt appropriate to include in the opening stage direction to his adaptation of *A Bond Honoured*), Osborne had nothing to say about this work other than that it had 'an absurd plot, some ridiculous characters, and some very heavy humour.' What he did to it was more drastic than anything usually contemplated by an adapter of the classics. He reduced it to less than a third of its length, made significant changes to the plot and characters, and grafted his own familiar obsessions on to the central protagonist.

There are losses to Lope's play that some people might find regrettable: the humour, for instance. In a work dominated by such a relentless killjoy as Leonido, one misses such touches of Lope as the dismay of Leonido's servant Tizón at the prospect of eating couscous in an Islamic country, or of being deprived there of wine ('I don't ask much from this miserable life, but I expect at least good wine, or any wine, for that matter'[3]).

More serious, because it distorts Lope's original intentions, is Osborne's handling of what he calls the play's 'Christian framework'. Though Osborne claims this as one of the two main reasons that attracted him to the work, he deals with it in slightly cursory, enigmatic fashion. In contrast to Lope, he has Leonido hang himself rather than emulate Christ's crucifixion; and he includes no hint of forgiveness or redemption. The satisfying balance of good and evil achieved by Lope is thus completely absent in Osborne's adaptation, which in turn means there is no real sense of a bond honoured. Tizón himself admits this in the work's caustic concluding line: 'It may not be a bond honoured, but it's a tune of sorts to end with.'

The main draw of the play to Osborne, and the only possible explanation why Tynan thought that the author of *Look Back in Anger* was the perfect person to adapt it, must surely have been 'the potentially fascinating dialectic with the principle character'.[4] Leonido, a man of demonic power whose birth is marked by the eruption of Etna, is someone seething with anger and violence. It is easy to understand how Osborne saw in him one of his typically cynical, disaffected protagonists whose pent-up fury has no real outlet. Osborne made him an even crueler person than the original Leonido, but did so with a language of punchy brilliance that captures all the energy and directness that are among the hallmarks of Lope's style. The resulting play, like the one on which it was based, might be a relatively minor work of his (and, despite the excellence of the original cast, it was a flop when first performed); but it remains an intriguing example of two playwrights speaking to each other across the centuries.

Whereas *A Bond Honoured* needed, in Osborne's view, radical tampering to make it come alive for modern audiences, *The Labyrinth of Desire* is an immediately accessible work of obvious present-day relevance.[5] This is one of those obscure plays of Lope that prove to be more original and interesting than several of those that are far better known. Translated here for the first time, and apparently unperformed in Spanish since the early seventeenth century, it is a fresh, wacky and utterly compelling comedy touching on female equality and sexual ambiguity. The time is surely right for a full-scale revival.

As with *A Bond Honoured*, it dates probably from some time between 1610 and 1616, a period marked in Lope's personal life by his permanent move to Madrid, the death of his second wife Juana de Guardo, and his taking up of the priesthood. In terms of the development of his plays, these were years characterized by a greater introspection, the predominance of female protagonists, and the abandonment of the action-packed plots so typical of his earlier works. These changes are exemplified in *The Labyrinth of Desire*. Though promising at first to be a straightforward courtly drama about love, revenge and honour (the first scene has the heroine Florela swearing to go off to Ferrara in search of the lover who has jilted her), it soon evolves into something much subtler and more complex. That it should end up in a real labyrinth imitative of that of Knossos is only too fitting for a work in which puzzles are constantly being presented, and whose sexual entanglements seem to mirror the emotional labyrinth that was Lope's own life.

'I am telling you the truth,' is the opening line of this play suitably fuelled by disguises and deceptions. The grand mistress of deceit is the exceptionally learned and intellectually razor-sharp Florela, the 'Mantuan Sybil', who, after moving to Ferrara, assumes the name Diana and talks her way into becoming the lady-in-waiting and confidante of the woman (Laura) whom her ex-lover Alexander (together with Italy's most eligible bachelors) is arduously courting. An extraordinarily close relationship develops between the two women, which takes on an even more intense nature when Florela, in a ploy to prevent

Laura taking up with Alexander, pretends she is really a man called Felix, and that she was forced to dress up in women's clothing as a result of a crime committed when she was a child. She also declares her passionate love for Laura.

There are numerous dramas from seventeenth century Spain in which men feign to be women, and vice versa, but none in which the erotic possibilities of the confusion are exploited to such an extent as they are here. The fact that Laura believes for most of the time that Florela is a man enables Lope to depict for the first time on the Spanish stage what must have struck audiences even then as a lesbian affair. The passion between them, of startling intensity, had surely a titillating effect, playing as it did on male sexual fantasies of seeing two women erotically engaged. An added edge to their love is given by Laura's occasional doubts about Florela's sexuality, which leads also to the play's most memorable line, 'Whatever sex or creature you might be, you are my God and the light of my existence.'

In this world of sexual ambivalence, in which a woman may or may not be a man, traditional views about male superiority become particularly nonsensical. One of the play's most absorbing moments is when Florela challenges Laura's suitors to debate the motion that 'women are no less capable than men in matters of government, war and the sciences'. What follows is probably the most sustained argument in favour of women's equality voiced in Spain before modern times; it is more remarkable still for dating from an age when women were officially considered by the Catholic Church to have no soul. Filled with references to Aristotle, St Thomas Aquinas, and other learned authorities, the debate might seem in the telling to be wordy, obscure and undramatic. But in fact it turns out to be both funny and theatrically thrilling. It is a testimony to Lope's popular touch that he is able to make light of his own formidable erudition; and it says much of his theatrical sense that he is able to turn a potentially turgid discussion into the verbal equivalent of a duel.

Only one man, the Spaniard Camacho, comes to Florela's defence as she parries thrusts from all directions. He is one of

Lope's supreme comic creations, and adds to this multi-textured work another key element of deception. Whereas Florela acts as a lady-in-waiting pretending to be a man, Camacho is a man-servant who takes on the part of an imaginary Spanish aristocrat. As earthy, commonsensical and food-obsessed as Lope's Tizón, he has the role of puncturing pretensions, intellectual, social and amorous. Against a background of mounting sexual intrigue and displays of ingenuity worthy of James Bond, he serves as a reminder of the human being that lies behind every mask. He ridicules those scholars who think that the mere donning of a gown makes them wiser and more erudite than ordinary mortals; and, through aping the aristocracy, he magnificently sends up courtly etiquette and customs. He is the only match to Florela.

As complex at times in its language as it is in its plot, *The Labyrinth of Desire* presents the translator with a dauntingly difficult task. The pun-riddled speeches of Camacho exemplify Lope's mastery of wordplay, while elsewhere there are passages of rhetorical magnificence and exquisite poetry: for instance, the overwhelming emotions unleashed during the momentous first meeting of Laura and Florela are conveyed in language of appropriately dazzling beauty. Lope was a notoriously fast writer, but some of the language employed here suggests a greater than usual care with words. To compound the problems for the translator, the play has survived only in a poorly punctuated edition that often makes it hard to read. There are lines whose exact meaning is likely to puzzle the most dedicated Lope scholar.

As with my previous translations of Lope de Vega, my essential concern has been to bring out the stunning immediacy and variety of tone so characteristic of this playwright. Though I have tried to be as faithful as possible to the original text, I have chosen not to be too pedantic or inflexible in my approach towards it. I have given the play a catchier and more contemporary title, condensed some scenes, and upheld the view that Lope's verse is best translated into prose, albeit into a prose that ranges from the colloquial to the poetically sonorous. I hope that the end result will awaken interest in what I believe to be one of the forgotten comic masterpieces of Golden Age Spain.

London, Autumn 2002

Acknowledgements

For help with some of the more impenetrable passages in *The Labyrinth of Desire*, I am greatly indebted to Robert Goodwin of King's College, London; Agustín de la Granja of Granada University; Matilde Javaloyes of the Cervantes Institute, London; Brígida Pastor of Glasgow University, and Carmen Suarez of Canning House, London. David Castillejo, whose invaluable *Las cuatrocientas obras de Lope* (Madrid, 1984) first drew my attention to this work, kindly read through my translation, and made useful suggestions. Amy Oliver allowed me the opportunity to see the play performed in a staged reading, while Colin Ellwood brought to bear on the work his usual insights and enthusiasm. The translation is dedicated to Fiona Bell.

Notes

1 *La fianza satisfecha* (c.1610–1616), Biblioteca de Autores Españoles, *Obras de Lope de Vega XII, Comedias de vidas de santos, IV*, ed. Marcelino Menéndez Pelayo, Madrid, 1965.
2 S Griswold Morley and Courtney Bruerton, *Cronología de las Comedias de Lope de Vega*, Editorial Gredos, 1968.
3 Biblioteca de Autores Españoles, *op.cit.*, p 127.
4 See Author's note, p.14.
5 The original Spanish title was *La prueba de los ingenios* (*The Testing of Wits*), Biblioteca de Autores Españoles, *op.cit.*, *Lope de Vega, Obras XXX*.

A BOND HONOURED

Author's Note

In 1963, Kenneth Tynan, Literary Manager of the National Theatre, asked me if I would adapt *La Fianza Satisfecha* by Lope de Vega. It was in three acts, had an absurd plot, some ridiculous characters and some very heavy humour. What did interest me was the Christian framework of the play and the potentially fascinating dialectic with the principal character. So I concentrated on his development (in the original he rapes his sister in the opening moments of the play without any preparatory explanation of his character or circumstances) and discarded most of the rest, reducing the play to one long act. *A Bond Honoured* is the result.

John Osborne

Characters

LEONIDO

TIZON
his servant

DIONISIO
his brother-in-law. Husband of Marcela

GERARDO
his father

BERLEBEYO
Moorish King

MARCELA
sister of Leonido

ZULEMA
a Moor

ZARRABULLI
a Moor

LIDORA
a Moorish Lady

MAID

SHEPHERD

A Bond Honoured was first performed at The National Theatre, London on 6 June 1966 with the following cast:

DIONISIO, Michael Byrne

BERLEBEYO, Graham Crowden

GERARDO, Paul Curran

LIDORA, Janina Faye

TIZON, Gerald James

MARCELA, Maggie Smith

LEONIDO, Robert Stephens

Director, John Dexter

Designer, Michael Annals

Musical Advisor, Marc Wilkinson

Act One
Scene 1: Sicily, Gerardo's Garden
Scene 2: Marcela's Bedchamber
Scene 3: Gerardo's Garden
Scene 4: Marcela's Bedchamber
Scene 5: Gerardo's Garden
Scene 6: Sicily. A beach

Act Two
Scene 1: Tunis
Scene 2: Tunis

ACT ONE

Scene 1

All the actors in the play sit immobile in a circle throughout most of the action. When those who are in the same scene rise to take part in it, they all do so together. Long cloaks should be worn. The acting style is hard to discover or describe. I will just say: it must be extremely violent, pent-up, toppling on and over the edge of animal howlings and primitive rage. At the same time, it should have an easy, modern naturalness, even in the most extravagant or absurd moments. It requires actors like athletes who behave like conversationalists. It is not impossible or as difficult as it sounds. We English are more violent than we allow ourselves to know. That is why we have the greatest body of dramatic literature in the world.

Sicily. GERARDO's garden by the sea. TIZON, a servant, lies asleep.

VOICE: (*Off.*) Tizon! Tizon!
  (*Enter LEONIDO.*)
LEONIDO: Tizon! Tizon – why, of course, of course
  asleep. All easy aren't you, snoozing? Like a basket of
  old laundry, mucky and no use to anyone. Wake up! Up!
TIZON: Master! I fell asleep.
LEONIDO: Tizon, when you sleep, you should do it under
  cover, in a hole or some cellar. Your sleeping's like your
  eating and most other things about you. It's better not
  looked on. When you just swallow a glass of wine the
  effect's like the dead stink of a bat dropped into a well.
  As for your other functions, I daren't think of them. But
  to find you *asleep,* all mess and remains like some
  decomposing beast, by the roadside, is so hateful to
  anyone awake to life itself, itself – you're lucky I didn't
  kill you.
TIZON: Forgive me.
LEONIDO: I can't forgive what I can't remake. Asleep!
  Why! You watch me when it suits your book.

TIZON: It was late, my lord.

LEONIDO: It's not late by my clock, and that is the one *you* live by. My heartbeat's the one you pay heed to. Your own's not worth keeping up for. You keep up for mine. It's more than you deserve, but it's what you've got and then you go and leave me when I'm alone and awake and waiting. Why? Eh?

TIZON: I was tired.

LEONIDO: Tired. Why? Tizon? – Are you tired?

TIZON: I don't know.

LEONIDO: No, you don't. Why should you be tired, you onlooker? You do nothing. And you're not furniture – nor decoration. There's no sweat in watching. I – I live for you, Tizon. You have nothing to do, nothing to expend. Busy little lard bundles should keep awake during the intervals and dull bits. Hear me! Keep awake and stay with me. And give me that wine. Is Dionisio gone yet?

TIZON: He's still with your father.

LEONIDO: How do you know, you don't even know you stink, you rumbling, drowsy equivocator?

TIZON : I –

LEONIDO: You don't. You're flailing aren't you?

TIZON: I am sure –

LEONIDO: No. Not *am* sure.

TIZON: I was watching –

LEONIDO: Am *not* sure.

TIZON: Master –

LEONIDO: You're dishonest, treacherous and you even botch treachery worse than most other men. Not *am* sure, Tizon.

TIZON: Yes.

LEONIDO: What?

TIZON: Yes, master.

LEONIDO: Yes, to what? What? Yes? You don't know. You back it as easily as 'no' if you think it'll come up. Don't know. Not watching – for once. The thing one should at least demand from a fool is stamina. Get up! (*Kicks him.*)

Tell me, no, not why, how, how can you sleep so much? Hey? When I've not slept for three nights?

TIZON: I don't know.

LEONIDO: Three nights since I slept and then only for a few minutes before I was tipped out by my sister.

TIZON: Sh!

LEONIDO: Sh what! Tipped out before her closing up time at dawn. What is it, why are you squinting and winking like some bit of bridal bait in the dark?

TIZON: My lord!

LEONIDO: You're like my sister. Ah, there's her light. Gone to bed already to get away from the tedium of her betrothed. Bridal bait. Marcela! Marcela! Gone to bed? Bridal bait!

TIZON: My lord, I beg you!

LEONIDO: Her maid's drawn her curtain. She sees herself as a bride guard too. What are you begging?

TIZON: Be circumspect.

LEONIDO: About?

TIZON: What may or may not in the past, that is, have occurred between you and your sister. Now that she's to be a bride –

LEONIDO: Not may or may not have. Has. Did. Is. Not was, might, may. *Is*. Well?

TIZON: It's unkind to pollute Dionisio's opinion of his bride. As well as your father's affection for his daughter –

LEONIDO: As for Dionisio' s minced opinions about my sister or any other object – they could only interest my father by their enormity of dullness.

TIZON: Then think of yourself, Leonido.

LEONIDO: Leonido, is it?

TIZON: Your reputation. I'm sorry.

LEONIDO: Don't be. Leonido was good for a moment. You almost creaked into life there, old fat bones, blown up bones, yes they are, why your bones have turned, so they have, they've simmered into gristle and jelly there, from all that sleep. From sleep that babyish dreaming in the belly that fishy swimming in mother's old moorings.

19

TIZON: Stop!

LEONIDO: Stop! Does your mother know you're back in there again?

TIZON: What is it? Do you want no man's good opinion.

LEONIDO: Not yours!

TIZON: No! Not mine.

LEONIDO: Good! First Leonido, now some more exertion. Is it only what the world thinks that stops your bones bubbling, eh?, in their dull stew and gets you to your feet? And answer me back? Now: nothing I have done has ever made me feel that anyone is better than I am. Though I was brought up to believe the reverse. See if Dionisio's still with my father. Why is it that of what they call the five Hindu hindrances you have only one: sloth? I have all the other four, craving, ill will, perplexity and restless brooding? I think that's right? Yes.

TIZON: They're still talking together.

LEONIDO: I could do with your sloth. Talking dowries and property and being important over my sister's body and disposing of it – as they think. So they think.

TIZON: If you have betrayed *Marcela's* virtue, you must keep it to yourself.

LEONIDO: You're as full of ifs as you are fleas. I've a harsh heart, Tizon, but don't sidle up to it or walk backwards away from it like my father does. That numb old nag now – he never took a difficult fence in his life either.

TIZON: He's an old man.

LEONIDO: He was born an old man. So was Dionisio. And you. All born dotards, and over-armoured. You need no protection from me.

TIZON: Need but not expect.

LEONIDO: Good. Don't expect. As for Marcela, she is the best part of the world for me. But she's not virtuous. No, not virtuous.

TIZON: She isn't now.

LEONIDO: She never was. I don't know what virtue is.
Can you tell me? I have never had any myself and I
never observed any in others either. You've none.

TIZON: You don't mean this.

LEONIDO: I *have* watched myself for signs of it, *I* promise
you. I am purblind to the needs of others just as they are
to mine. Your laughter may be my pleasure but your
howlings might be too. I've set traps and tried to catch
myself out in a virtuous act, but I've never done what
people call a good thing that didn't give me pleasure.
What ill-service can I do myself? What affection have I
ever felt that didn't run home back to me at the end of
the day? *Who* do I like? Or love? No one. Myself? A
little. But not much, I'm not much lovable. Although I
am preferable to anyone that is. For me I detest clever
men and dullards. I could roast and baste them slowly
myself and read a book at the same time or top and tail a
virgin. Or something. Simple men are too content and
ambitious men are ambitious and ambitions too simple
to be tolerated, tolerated or countenanced by *anyone* – at
least who has ever sat down quietly and consistently and
decently schooled themselves in pain. For their own
pleasure? Well – there's more mettle in painful pleasure
even than, than the restraints of over-protected and
feeble men like them – those two there. You see, there, it
all flies back to *pleasure,* like stooping falcon. Pleasure in
self, shallow self, cracked and wormy as I may be. You're
the same, Tizon. Surprised. We're no different, you and I.
I *am* somewhat swifter at the kill. Always and every time.
Will be. And forever more. There is no disinterest in
nature. And good and evil are men's opinions of
themselves.

TIZON: Dionisio's leaving.

LEONIDO: Good. *Why* do you watch me, Tizon?

TIZON: I am your servant.

LEONIDO: Can you, can you tell me the truth?

TIZON: I try.

LEONIDO: How can you be honest? You are cursed with dishonest eyes. Yes. It should be a handicap in a servant, but! Dare say it gets overlooked. Not noticed. They're full of blood, as usual. Have you looked at them? Poor pink, pink, not red, mark you pink lines. And meanness and envy, envy most of all. The will to wound but no will, lackey's eyes, traced indelicately, not attractively. Loaded with shame, shame and the dread of punishment... No wonder I avoid your eyes. Why do you watch me?

TIZON: No servant tells the truth.

LEONIDO: Right! Nor could. Is the old man gone to bed?

TIZON: Yes.

LEONIDO: Very well. I think then...I shall go up to my sister. Well? Servant. Were you about to say something?

TIZON: No, my lord.

LEONIDO: My lord again. And what will *you* do while I am awake upstairs? Niffy dormouse?

TIZON: I shall wait.

LEONIDO: Not doze?

TIZON: No.

LEONIDO: No? Dozy?

TIZON: No.

LEONIDO: You'll doze. One day you *shall*. And who knows when that is? And perhaps you'll want to then? However...wait. You may get some more pleasure from me before then. So my sister's waiting... Her light burns. Not over brightly but it burns. Just about to put it out...but I'll be there before then. Sisters are there to be trapped, Tizon. Tripped up. And over she goes. We'll talk again soon? I doubt I'll be sleeping much tonight, or if I do, something will waken me. Try not to doze.
(*He goes. TIZON stays awake.*)

Scene 2

MARCELA's bedchamber. MARCELA in her nightgown with her MAID. The MAID looks out of the window.

MAID: He's gone.

MARCELA: Who?

(*Enter LEONIDO.*)

LEONIDO: Why, Dionisio.

MAID: My lord!

LEONIDO: Gone. And so may you be now. Get along.

MAID: My lady is about to sleep.

LEONIDO: My lady is about to talk.

MAID: Sir!

LEONIDO: With me! We are not strangers to one another. You must know that there's a matter of blood between us. And between *us?* Please: the door.

MAID: Goodnight, lady!

(*He thrusts her out.*)

LEONIDO: Goodnight. And how *is* my lady then?

MARCELA: Prepared for sleep.

LEONIDO: Well, prepare yourself for bed first. All this sleeping. Your betrothed has gone off – to sleep too, no doubt.

MARCELA: I would rather you did not bawl up at my window.

LEONIDO: Bawl?

MARCELA: Ay! Bawl! Bridal bait!

LEONIDO: Bridal bait! This is your brother, chicken. Come along! Look at me now. What is it? Aren't I allowed to bait you?

MARCELA: Leave me.

LEONIDO: Make me.

MARCELA: You bait to kill.

LEONIDO: Not you.

MARCELA: Yes. Me. You were never playful.

LEONIDO: I have played with you, Marcela, since the day you were born.

MARCELA: To win or wound. Which you always do.

LEONIDO: How did you leave your betrothed?

MARCELA: Well.

LEONIDO: And easily?

MARCELA: He's angry with you.

LEONIDO: I may sleep tonight yet. The thought of Dionisio's anger would make an owl yawn. Well?

MARCELA: He complains you have lied all over Sicily that he's a bastard. That his mother was a whore and a crone and the only woman who has died in childbed of old age.

LEONIDO: Does this sound like my invention?

MARCELA: Yes.

LEONIDO: There! It made you smile.

MARCELA: Well: He has not the edge himself to make such a fancy, I admit.

LEONIDO: I may have said something.

MARCELA: Something? What was it?

LEONIDO: I don't know. About old bitches dropping runts only. But bastard no. Dionisio is *legitimate*. He's lawful as an endless sermon. That's not to say proceedings shouldn't be taken up against him for being born at all. No, for certain he is in the common run of legitimacy. A bastard's common too, but a bastard you see's separate, a weed, often strong, quite powerful. Like your Charlemagne, your King Arthur, your Gawain, your Roland and your Irish kings. There! You're smiling at me. It *is* fun, not repentance makes remission of sins.

MARCELA: There's none of either in you. Or ever will be.
(*He mauls her.*)
Go to your own bed, Leonido! You are mad.

LEONIDO: This is one of my lucid patches.
(*They kiss. She stops struggling.*)

MARCELA: Stop! You have a tongue like a lizard.

LEONIDO: There are a great many flies in your gullet. They should be got out. Otherwise you will choke.
(*He kisses her again.*)

MARCELA: Blow out the light…that's better.

LEONIDO: Now you're close to me again, Marcela. Marcela... When you look coldly on me, I think my bowels will break... Marcela... Marcela...

MARCELA: Yes?

LEONIDO: I can't see your face... What defect is there in me? I find beauty and comfort...and sustenance...only... in you. There's no light from the sea tonight. I can't see your face. I don't care what people may speculate. I do *not* want them to know. Not words or movements or moments. Those are for our pleasure, only. Marcela? Secrecy *is* the nerve of love. Can you see me? Marcela? Are you asleep...?

Scene 3

GERARDO's garden. DIONISIO sits with his bride, MARCELA, on the terrace by the sea. TIZON lies drunk among the flowers. Enter GERARDO with LEONIDO, who kicks TIZON as he passes.

GERARDO: I cannot understand you.

LEONIDO: Or young men like me.

GERARDO: Or young men like you.

LEONIDO: Whoever *they* may be. Only old men seem to have the good fortune to meet them.

GERARDO: What?

LEONIDO: Go on, father, you talk endless doggerel as if it were the poetry of revealed doctrine. But go on. It's your privilege.

GERARDO: *You* are too privileged. In my time –

LEONIDO: As if now wasn't his time –

GERARDO: – time it was all war and uncertainty. Now everything is easy come by and you and those like you hang about sniffing blood ungratefully and harrying everyone and everything in your rancorousness.

LEONIDO: Old men inhabit what are clear for miles as fortresses all their lives and talk as if they were pigging it in mud huts.

GERARDO: What?

LEONIDO: There's no cutting a way through your hairy old ear. Is there? I say that clapper tongue of yours has deafened you inside that hollow bell. Hollow bell.

GERARDO: Bell. Wedding bell?

LEONIDO: Bedding well. Yes. Very soon from the look of them. Your head, father, the top, there, where your cap screws on, you rancid old jar.

GERARDO: You are too full of contempt.

LEONIDO: I take in a fresh stock twice weekly and whenever I am with *you.*

GERARDO: Do you hear?

LEONIDO: Alas, my ears are *not* overgrown with old man's moss. Could you not clean up that old garden to your brain one day, father? It might not be easier to enter but it might be more pleasant for the rest of us.

GERARDO: You tread upon your sister's bridal gown. You abuse her husband. You hiss dislike and envy at the priest. I think your midriff and your backbone must be full of – serpents.

LEONIDO: They'd be useful worms for dim dogs like the priest – or, indeed, you, father. I say! At least, they stop me growing fat on commonplaces.

GERARDO: See, there. Look there. Your sister still weeps at the remembrance of your cruelty. All her days, I dare say. And on her wedding day.

LEONIDO: Or at the yawning expectation of her wedding night. Or the expectation of her yawning wedding night. Tizon? What? Retiring already, Marcela!

MARCELA: I am tired and unwell.

LEONIDO: Who has made you unwell then? Dionisio?

DIONISIO: You shall not come near her again, Leonido. I have told her. Nor enter our house ever.

LEONIDO: Not welcome? Nowhere? Marcela?

MARCELA: Nowhere.

LEONIDO: Never?

MARCELA: No.

GERARDO: Come, child. Take her to bed, Dionisio. It's best. Your brother has not altogether blighted this day for you, and thank heavens, the night is not in his hands. My blessings on you both and be at peace together while you may. And remember Father Augustine.

MARCELA: 'Our heart is restless till it finds itself in thee.'

GERARDO: Good, child. Take her, Dionisio.

LEONIDO: Why you've been busy, bride, you've been gospelling and swapping pieties with the priest.

MARCELA: We prayed together.

DIONISIO: All night.

LEONIDO: You'll not be up so long, so don't hurry. So! This is why you are so feverish – from sitting out in a devotional draught. That's why her bed was empty!

MARCELA: I was not seeking your permission. And, Leonido, listen from this time: I obey only my husband.

GERARDO: There, Leonido. Embrace it, and off with you.

MARCELA: Goodnight, father.

GERARDO: Goodnight, my child.

(*They turn.*)

LEONIDO: Marcela? (*Pause.*) Goodnight.

(*She stares coldly, grasps DIONISIO's hand and goes into the house. GERARDO regards him for a moment, then follows them. Music. LEONIDO stands stricken. Presently, TIZON hands him a flagon of wine to drink from. LEONIDO takes it and drinks.*)

So. Rome has spoken. The matter is settled.

TIZON: That's the way of it, my lord. That's the way *of* it.

LEONIDO: What's the way of what? Must you look out at the sea and not here? There's nothing stirring out there.

TIZON: Quietly, my lord. They are joined together now –

LEONIDO: And by what dishonest mortar.

TIZON: You must accept it.

LEONIDO: I accept nothing. Nothing is offered.

TIZON: Her light is on.

LEONIDO: Not for me…it isn't…being looked on as a good bargain…Gerardo! Do you hear me now! I always worked for passion rather than for profit, for the salt pearls that ran down the knots of her spine. Marcela!

(*He stares up at MARCELA's window. More music. TIZON drops off. LEONIDO draws his sword. He strikes him with it. TIZON is brought to his feet by the sudden pain.*)

Draw! Draw!

(*Confused, TIZON does so. They duel. LEONIDO's rage helps him to beat TIZON quickly and he has his sword pointing at his belly.*)

There!

(*TIZON goes.*)

One day, one day of your lifetime I shall kill you with this sword. Now? No. Tonight or tomorrow or in a year. Whenever you affront me most or I'm most impatient. Don't misjudge the time by my mood. It may be when I'm gasping for want of enemies or running idly up to a joke… See how alert you must be! You'd better keep awake while you can. After all, that alone, that incessant discipline, will add to your span. It must do so. Now, isn't that a fierce, energetic structure for a man to be alive in. That'll keep you awake. It'll keep you *occupied*. You won't *dare* sleep. Or perhaps you will. We'll see. It may not matter to you, it may come, it may not. Now you're breathing, now you're bleeding. Ah! *Never* turn your back on me. Or look away. *Watch* me, Tizon. And now I shall spoil the bride's sleep. You may as well wait a while. Relax yourself a little.

(*He takes a lamp and goes, leaving TIZON to wipe the blood from his face.*)

Scene 4

MARCELA's bedchamber. Enter LEONIDO with lamp. MARCELA in bed.

MARCELA: Dionisio?

LEONIDO: No – Leonido!

MARCELA: I beg you to leave me. Brother, you have had the best of me.

LEONIDO: And you of me.

MARCELA: Well! Now leave the rest to Dionisio. It's little enough but the best for all of us.

LEONIDO: At last! You confess it was the best!

MARCELA: I confess it to flatter you, to be rid of you before my husband returns.

LEONIDO: Are you so hot for this husband's – *hus*band – husband's jobbery? Is there no more, sweetheart? Please?

MARCELA: Ask me no explanations. There is no more. I have nothing for you.

LEONIDO: Marcela. We have been conspirators. Can you deny it? We have never thought of winning – only of each other. I thought of us only as two children together. (*She laughs.*)

Anything, any excess is preferable to this miserable subordination, this imposture, this –

MARCELA: Go!

LEONIDO: This low – low, uterine appeasement!

MARCELA: Dionisio!

LEONIDO: It is only in you that I see a foot ahead of me and my heartbeat recovers. What is it now? A life of scavenging for slops of your attention. Eh? Upturned from the window to your bedchamber? Remember, my mouth, my mouth, your mouth, Marcela.

MARCELA: A man cannot make a wife of his sister. It's bane for both of them. Don't ask me why. Ask the world or God, or what, but there's law and nature against you in their battalions. Now go, my dear, I am afraid enough already.

LEONIDO: Marcela, I am a woman's son. Your mother's son. I love women. Shall I *tell* you? No? Why? Sister: when did you ever look for me as I looked for you?

MARCELA: Always.

(*They kiss.*)

Dionisio! He's coming!

LEONIDO: Sister, what has this man done…to you? He has laid his mark on you. You are healed somehow and hardened. Where's your blood now? Your lap is as

wooden as a bench. You *will* not, no, *not,* sweetheart, not
deprive me? Take off your shift.
(*LEONIDO begins stripping MARCELA, who screams.
DIONISIO enters.*)

MARCELA: Dionisio! My God, *help* me!
(*The men duel. DIONISIO falls. LEONIDO strikes
MARCELA with his sword and goes. MARCELA goes to
DIONISIO as he recovers.*)

Scene 5

*GERARDO's garden. Enter LEONIDO with bloody sword. He grins
at TIZON.*

LEONIDO: It's done.

TIZON: But not well. Was it?

LEONIDO: No, not well this time, but let's say we
celebrated all the occasions past when it *was* well done.

TIZON: Have you no feeling? Even for reckoning?

LEONIDO: I have God's credit for the moment. Let him
settle up for me, and send in his account when he wants
to. He must know my credit's good, indeed. He has
never – in his eternal life – had a client with better
prospects or security. Nor ever will have. Come. I'm
bored here. Let's go.

TIZON: Where?

LEONIDO: We'll have a late stroll in the market place.
You'll enjoy that. And you will sleep all the better for it.

TIZON: You want to show off your sister's blood in the
market place.

LEONIDO: Oh, you think I killed her?

TIZON: Didn't you?

LEONIDO: No. I added a few grace notes to her face.

TIZON: God gave her one face and a good one, and you
add to it! Like mine. Don't you think you'll pay for all
this handiwork of yours.

LEONIDO: I'll tell you: send the bill in to God. I'll settle
with him later. Don't concern yourself, Tizon. You'll lose
your sleep.

TIZON: For the final settling up! I will stay awake. I promise you.

LEONIDO: Good, Tizon. I do believe I've smoked out your torpor. For tonight run! With me! Come! Here's the old man with the other. Oh – breathless with survival too.

(*They hide. Enter GERARDO and DIONISIO.*)

Nasty palaverer. He's woken the old pudding from his prayers.

DIONISIO: How can I tell you?

LEONIDO: How indeed?

DIONISIO: I came upon them together. Together, my wife, his sister and both of them your children. It's quite famous the kind of man he is, but I thought I was secure on this occasion. But I was wrong. Señor. I blame you. Yes, you. You have not checked him as you could have done and now we all suffer for it. He has stolen from us all, from you, from his sister, and now from me. Look at my face!

GERARDO: Marcela. Did she defend herself?

DIONISIO: As well as she could. And now she has a striped face like mine to show for it.

GERARDO: Oh, Leonido!

DIONISIO: Nothing will change him. I shall hunt him down.

(*LEONIDO appears.*)

LEONIDO: Hunt me down then.

GERARDO: What have you done with my daughter?

DIONISIO: Not what he set out for.

LEONIDO: Not on *this* evening. However: it is true I have left some equipment somewhere – sometime – in that particular warren.

(*DIONISIO draws.*)

It is true, father, I tried to rob her – honour on this special night. Not because she wanted me to but because that is how *I* was born. By the same brutality. As you well know. With any good fortune I shall still insult her blood and yours too and take away what little honour you have creasing beneath your mattress. I did it not because it was good but interesting. I am glad to see it's painful to both of you.

GERARDO: Leonido. Why must you do these things to us? You are pillaging my heart. For all his mercy, the good God must punish you with the miseries of hell. Oh, if I could be wrong in that.

LEONIDO: Then be comforted. The precedents for your prognostications are most encouraging.

(*DIONISIO lunges at LEONIDO.*)

Out of the way, old man.

GERARDO: You call me old man because you have darkened the name father. Because you know you deserve no father nor even to mouth the word.

LEONIDO: So! You want my attention!

(*He strikes him. GERARDO cries out.*)

DIONISIO: Father, you'll be revenged.

LEONIDO: If I fix a place, will you trust me?

DIONISIO: Yes, even you.

LEONIDO: You must not expect more or better of me… My fingers are like quills. Read the message on your face… Very well. I can't bear to look on that any longer. If it's revenge then, let us say sunset. By the seashore. Tonight.

(*He goes.*)

GERARDO: Humble him, oh God! I am too infirm. Let some Moorish lance skewer my own son. May they drag him on a halter into Tunis, a bruised litter of flesh strung behind some fleeing camel!

DIONISIO: Be calm, father. You have a new son here. In me. Take a little pleasure in your son and daughter and what's to come from both of them. Let me lift you. There. On my shoulder. There.

GERARDO: Let's go to see your wife, my daughter. Your grief is mine just as she is mine.

DIONISIO: There, father. Come.

GERARDO: Let the world judge these two men. I ask no more of it. Nothing.

Scene 6

Sicily. A beach. LEONIDO lies sleeping. Enter KING
BERLEBEYO, ZULEMA and ZARRABULLI.

KING: Praise Allah. Sicilian sand! Feel it.

ZULEMA: As you commanded, oh King.

ZARRABULLI: We can snare all the Christians we can
   carry home here, and then back off to Tunis.

KING: I wish they'd appear. If it were not for Lidora, I'd be
   at home. Where are we?

ZULEMA: This is the port of Alicarte. And this is the
   beach of Saso. Christians come here, I promise you, my
   King.

ZARRABULLI: Take care you are not converted. They are
   great wheedlers.

ZULEMA: Here's one: he's asleep.

KING: Take his sword.

ZULEMA: Ah!

   (*He takes it.*)

KING: Now wake him.

LEONIDO: Why, you black lard!

KING: Tie his hands.

LEONIDO: I can see, sir, you have not been to Sicily
   before. Here then.

   (*He grabs branch from a tree.*)

KING: *Kill* him, Zulema! Kill the Christian!

LEONIDO: Kill the Christian! Kill the Moor!

   (*They fight. LEONIDO fights like a madman and disarms*
   them all.)

KING: I surrender! Surrender! I never, anywhere, saw such
   strength. I am your slave, and if it is your pleasure, I
   think it will be mine. Who are you?

LEONIDO: I will tell you. But drink this wine first.

KING: I don't drink wine.

LEONIDO: Drink: King.

   (*He drinks.*)

   Well, Moor. King Berlebeyo, oh, I know you. I was born
   in Alicarte, by the river Saso near the mountains of

Petralia. They say that when my mother gave birth to me, the whole island heard it and her breasts were covered in blood, as a sign of hatred, you see, and Etna, yes, Etna erupted, and the only contented soul here was my own. They were frightened of me from the first. Not that I killed anyone. Only wished to. They were all consumed with process. Had no idea of the unique. Me, I had an overstrong instinct, you understand and this is an island of over protected people. The range of possibilities in living here shrinks with every year. Soon, it will be every week, then daily. I am a liar. Lying is inescapable to me. I understand a liar and I cherish a thief. I think I have raped thirty women and I don't include my mother, who hardly resisted. My sister took to it regularly and easily except on her wedding night. Why I don't know. Something is wrong. God or myself. But then: I stabbed her twice in the face, oh yes, and her husband. I could fatten *him* up for you. And then there was the man who calls himself my father, but no more, I dare say. That pleased me more than all the rest. So, you see, proud Moor, *you* are the tail end.

KING: Valiant and noble Leonido, by the sacred temple where lies the holy and divine body of Mahomet, although I am ashamed of capture and am heir to a Kingdom, I rejoice in being your captive. I come here to please a Moorish lady whom I long for. Her name is Lidora and she asked me for a Sicilian Christian, even though she has more than she knows what to do with. So I come. And found my master.

LEONIDO: Then we shall take you back to Lidora, eh? All of us. Drink. Go on.

KING: If I do – Mahomet will punish me.

LEONIDO: Refer him – to me.

(*He drinks.*)

There–we shall get on. Now: give me a cloak and turban.

(*Enter TIZON. He watches in horror.*)

Ah, Tizon. Help me with these.

ZARRABULLI: Master! It is *my* task.

(*ZARRABULLI and ZULEMA robe him in Moorish costume.
The others watch.*)

LEONIDO: What do you think, Tizon?

(*He lunges.*)

Dozing, Tizon! Do I make a good Moor? When do you think you'll die?

TIZON: You make a grand Turk. A Suliman –

LEONIDO: Go and tell my father this – I renounce his blood. Also his God, his law, the baptism and the sacraments, oh yes, and the Passion and Death. I think I shall follow Mahomet.

TIZON: Leonido! How can you ask me? I dare not take such a message.

LEONIDO: Dare not! Well, then –

TIZON: No – I'll take it.

LEONIDO: Yes.

KING: May you wear this and live forever, Leonido!

LEONIDO: And you too. And now let us go and see this Lidora.

KING: I am your slave.

LEONIDO: And my master.

TIZON: I will go then. Think on this, Leonido.

LEONIDO: I don't think. But I shall observe my processes as well as I can.

TIZON: I'll take this long cloak of yours and hat as witnesses of what's happened. Remember: you have a debt to pay to heaven.

LEONIDO: And remember also: I have the best bond. Let the Good Lord pay pound for pound. I'll settle later.

(*Exit.*)

ACT TWO

Scene 1

Tunis. Enter LEONIDO in Moorish costume. With him LIDORA, a Moorish lady.

LIDORA: Stop.

LEONIDO: Why?

LIDORA: Turn and face me.

LEONIDO: But I've no wish to face you.

LIDORA: You are cruel.

LEONIDO: It comes easily if you apply yourself to it.

LIDORA: I love you.

LEONIDO: Me?

LIDORA: You.

LEONIDO: Or my cruelty is it? What if I'm not for the asking?

LIDORA: I shall die.

LEONIDO: Now or later?

LIDORA: On your account.

LEONIDO: So you keep saying.

LIDORA: Great Argolan!

LEONIDO: Lidora?

LIDORA: Won't you love me?

LEONIDO: I've no need, nor the energy or curiosity.

LIDORA: Oh, you are cruel.

LEONIDO: Yes, and you're a fool. I am only one of them but you can be both.

LIDORA: Dearest!

LEONIDO: I am weary of your Moorish yapping and haggling. Now leave me.

LIDORA: Does my beauty mean nothing to you?

LEONIDO: The sun hasn't burned up my head even if it has yours. To me: you are no more beautiful than some overheated whelp trailing strangers in the bazaar. I have

36

loved oh, many women, Lidora, or performed, I suppose, the rituals of it passably well. I allow then that you're beautiful and you can take some pride in that, though not much. Beauty is just one of many wells you might have been dropped in when your mother bore you. And all Moorish women bore me. Oh, there's a great deal of display in you, but I think it promises too much. There's a trick in there, possibly hundreds of them, and that, Lidora, is repellent. To me.

LIDORA: I am Moorish but I too hate Moors. I have much to give you. I know it. Love me, Argolan.

(*Enter the KING.*)

KING: Is this how you observe the King's law?

LIDORA: When did I not heed your law?

KING: Why, by trying to enlist proud Argolan here as one of your lovers. Now.

LIDORA: What offence is there in that then?

KING: There is this offence: you swore that when I brought you a Christian you would love me.

LIDORA: True. But you are not betrayed yet. Besides, for all that, what Christian did you bring back? You brought back a *Moor* and I am in love with him. I would give him my heart's blood if he asked for it.

LEONIDO: Don't be rash, Lidora. Heart's blood adds relish to a dull, many a dull dish.

LIDORA: I would give him more than relish. I love him even for the clothes he wears and his renunciation. If he were still Christian I should love him.

(*Exit.*)

KING: Well, Argolan. What do you say?

LEONIDO: It's a common pattern. The more she protests, the less I want to hear about it. When I love this woman, Mahomet will no longer be a holy prophet, Berlebeyo.

KING: For this favour you are doing me, Argolan, you shall see the true art and scope of the great love I bear for you. Tunis is yours. Demand whatever you want of it. My Kingdom is yours.

LEONIDO: I don't want someone else's kingdom.

KING: Try on my crown.

LEONIDO: I'll not go shares. *If* I wear your crown one day, it shall be in my own Kingdom.

KING: Are you mad? Remember: you have left your own homeland behind.

LEONIDO: A sprightly old cock will crow anywhere he likes. Call on your government, King. Call on your city. Call out Mahomet. I am going to eat you! Out, Moor, out with your sword!

KING: Lidora!

(*Enter LIDORA.*)

LIDORA: What's this?

LEONIDO: The one you love. I shall bust your law, break your city, strike at friendship and kill your King. I'll wait for you by the river.

(*Exit.*)

KING: Rot you, you dog!

LIDORA: Wait. Wait, noble Berlebeyo. Check yourself.

KING: What?

LIDORA: Swallow your bitterness. It's acid that runs through dwarfs. For the love of me, and yourself, pardon him.

KING: If you wish it. But only then, then I will. I cannot see for anger, nor can I now, only you and your love can rein me in. Hold me in. Hold me. There!

LIDORA: May Mahomet strengthen you forever.

(*Enter ZARRABULLI.*)

ZARRABULLI: Lidora, what is the reward for good news?

KING: Bargains after. LIDORA: Tell us.

ZARRABULLI: Zulema is at the gates with as many Christian prisoners as you'd wish for.

LIDORA: Oh! Is it true?

ZARRABULLI: They are Sicilians.

LIDORA: Tell him to come in.

ZARRABULLI: He is very Pompey.

KING: He's a fine soldier.

(*Enter ZULEMA, GERARDO, TIZON and MARCELA – prisoners.*)

ZULEMA: Come in, Christians. Kiss King Berlebeyo's feet. And you, my lord, put your foot in their mouths. And in mine.

LIDORA: Oh, you have excelled yourself! Tell me what has happened.

ZULEMA: I have been lucky, as you shall see.

LIDORA: Tell me.

ZULEMA: Lidora, I set out happily from Tunis, with no thought but of your pleasure, with a hundred Moors. After weeks on the water, I made out the high walls of Sicily, packed with those people who follow this cross, followers of the naked prophet, who they say is on nodding terms with God. I landed, split my men into bands and looked for the quarry. In the darkness we saw nothing, but at dawn on the foreshore Allah rewarded us for the night with three men and one woman. One of the men I spliced with my cutlass to clear the air and the remainder are here before you. Three fine Sicilians for your pleasure.

LIDORA: You have pleased me so much, so exceedingly, I can think of only one gift adequate.

ZULEMA: Lidora: you offer me more than any conquest I have ever made.

LIDORA: You're worthy of it.

KING: Divine Mahomet. Do you give yourself to anyone for a gift.

ZULEMA: I think, great lord, *your* claim is undisputed. Forgive me. Let Lidora keep this gift. I remain your slave. I meant only to give you, my lord, delight through her.

KING: She does not deserve Christians for servants but Mahomet himself. Zulema, I present this ring to you. Take it but not for payment. As a sign of affection.

ZULEMA: On another expedition I will do better. For you both. You shall have the Eastern church on one hand, the Western on the other. Roman and Eastern shall touch the soles of your feet.

TIZON: So much talk and no wine with it, ever.

LIDORA: With your leave, lord, I'll send for Argolan.

KING: Wait till I have gone.

ZULEMA: Have you fallen out?

LIDORA: It is over now. Argolan is coming back to us.

ZULEMA: Then he can meet his countrymen.

KING: Find him.

ZULEMA: I shall go. I only wish to serve you.

LIDORA: I know how you should be repaid.

(*He goes.*)

KING: I will leave you alone. I've no fancy for any of these.

(*He goes.*)

LIDORA: What is the matter? Why are you weeping? Remember you don't yet know whose power you have fallen into. Even though you are prisoners, you must not look like this. Your face is beautiful. Let me look at it.

MARCELA: Oh noble and beautiful Moor. It is not for myself. What moves me is the condition of this old man. His dignity and wisdom are the world's luck. If I should serve you, it'll not matter. I know how to bear things, and I hope you will be patient with me. But how can this man serve you when he has such a short time to live. How, Señora, can he be of use when he is worn out. What pleasure can you take in these powdery bones? He is certain to displease and irritate. Punish me for his fault, I beg you, even twice as much. If the father errs, then let the daughter pay, Señora, let the daughter pay.

LIDORA: No more. Now I beg *you*. Wipe your eyes. What is your name?

MARCELA: Marcela.

LIDORA: Calm yourself, Marcela. Your father may be a prisoner, but he has found another daughter.

MARCELA: Señora.

LIDORA: Old man. Embrace me, old man.

(*GERARDO weeps.*)

Our love is clasped in this for good. Hold me closer. Ask him for me, Marcela, for he will listen to you. Even if all Tunis rises up, I will affirm today that I have met my father. Are you happy to be father to me?

GERARDO: I will be your slave.

LIDORA: Put up a front before the Moors and lift your head a little. Stop crying, Marcela. We are sisters. Truly.

TIZON: What about me? Who lifts my head for me?
(*Enter LEONIDO.*)

LEONIDO: Well? Ah Tizon! You have woken in a strange place.

LIDORA: I wanted only to please you, Argolan.

LEONIDO: And I wished to please you. So?

MARCELA: Dear God, what have I done to you to set me under him again!

LIDORA: I wanted to show how much I adore you, Argolan. These prisoners, all Christians, have just been given to me by Zulema. They all serve me, and I want you to know, they will serve you with me.
(*GERARDO goes to kiss the sole of LEONIDO's feet.*)
May it please Allah!

LEONIDO: I will treat you all as you deserve. Are you honoured to be at my feet? Heaven casts you down just as it casts me up. You at my feet, yes, you paltry old toad. I'll not have your mouth near any shoe of mine, or I'll have to burn it afterwards. Get up! You're a brave groveller. Own the earth do you? Do you?
(*He kicks GERARDO in the mouth.*)
Get up!

GERARDO: Oh, divine heaven!

TIZON: You struck him on his knees.

LEONIDO: Why not. It's his natural posture.

GERARDO: This is what a good father suffers from a bad son.

LIDORA: Father, get up, get up. I put myself in your hands. What is happening between you?

GERARDO: Oh, bad son.

LEONIDO: I your son? Utter the name son again to me and I'll hook your jaw to the rafters.

MARCELA: What have I done to you, Leonido?

LEONIDO: Do you know me?

MARCELA: I never knew you! Why don't you kill me – Moor?

LEONIDO: Mahomet will have his vengeance on you both.
    You won't find protection here.
LIDORA: Father, sit down, sit down in this chair.
MARCELA: *Moor,* do as you like. Do as you like.
LEONIDO: Oh, Marcela. I've waited for you.
MARCELA: But take care.
LIDORA: Come to my arms, Señor.
GERARDO: Do not weep, child. I am better.
    (*Sits.*)
MARCELA: Take care, Leonido.
    (*LEONIDO takes out his dagger.*)
LEONIDO: Father? Father?
GERARDO: Yes?
LEONIDO: Do your old eyes see this?
GERARDO: They do.
LEONIDO: Then they still see very well.
    (*He strikes GERARDO in the eyes. GERARDO covers them
    with a cloth.*)
MARCELA: Lidora, hold him!
LEONIDO: Now you can see less than you ever chose to
    see.
LIDORA: What jungle did you spring from. Oh!
LEONIDO: Kiss this blade, old man. Down, go on! Your
    daughter wants me to kill you in her own way. Marcela,
    do your duty by me. Yes? Or watch the old toad croak.
MARCELA: There's no answering you. I can't.
GERARDO: Don't be doubtful, Marcela. Better that I
    should die than you should be his lover.
LEONIDO: Does either matter?
GERARDO: I will not have her dishonoured.
LEONIDO: Answer?
MARCELA: Kill him.
LEONIDO: So!
MARCELA: Wait!
GERARDO: Don't lose heart, daughter.
LEONIDO: He'd best die. I assure you.
MARCELA: Die then! No!
LEONIDO: Speak up, sister.

MARCELA: I want him to die.

LEONIDO: Ah!

MARCELA: Not to die!

LEONIDO: You're in some difficulty?

(*She covers her eyes but LEONIDO makes her watch.*)

Now!

MARCELA: Now?

LEONIDO: And on your daughter's head!

GERARDO: Follow him, Marcela. Follow him.

MARCELA: Then do it.

LEONIDO: Do it?

MARCELA: Yes.

LIDORA: Argolan!

(*She holds him back.*)

LEONIDO: By the Koran, Argolan will have you *for* dessert. But Tunis shall burn first. TUNIS FIRST. (*He goes.*)

Scene 2

Tunis. Enter LEONIDO, distracted, like a madman. A voice interrupts now and then as he speaks.

LEONIDO: Marcela!

VOICE: Lidora.

LEONIDO: Marcela. I feel the bond tightening. Yes, it's tightening.

VOICE: Calm.

LEONIDO: Beyond logic so beyond doubt. Marcela, miserable, deluded and deluding family. Where are you? Where's your timorous Dionisio? Where is your *memory* of me? It shall soon fail. My imprint will have died out of all hearts inside a month. Discard. A discard. I have been mostly, a fair mixture of intelligence, mostly, self-criticism and, yes, gullibility. Yes, that's a hesitating assessment.

VOICE: Hesitate.

LEONIDO: But there's a hint in it.

VOICE: Hint.

LEONIDO: Allah! God! Marcela. Gullibility, self-criticism. Such people are always identifying, scrabbling for their stars, for signs in themselves, in the latest philosophy twice a week. If you have no dreams or portents for the day, they will knock one up for you. If you have not hit your wife or thought of killing your father. Mother. Daughter. Son. They will think you impoverished, or insensible. You will be made to dream again. I want no more dreams.

VOICE: For that which I do.

LEONIDO: I allow not. For what I would, that I do not. But what I hate: that I do. I know that in me.

VOICE: In my flesh.

LEONIDO: There is no good thing. For the will is present in me. But how to perform what is good. I...

VOICE: Not.

LEONIDO: For the good thing I would, I do not... But the evil: that I do. So then I find the law. When I do good evil is present in me. For I delight in the law of God after the inward man. But I see another law in my members, warring against the law of my mind, and bringing me into captivity.

VOICE: To the law of sin.

LEONIDO: Which of my members? Who shall deliver me? (*Enter SHEPHERD barefoot.*)

SHEPHERD: Cannot a hard heart soften?

LEONIDO: Ay, soften. That will do. Soften is the course.

SHEPHERD: Curse.

LEONIDO: It's you. You, who spoke. Who are you?

SHEPHERD: I am a shepherd.

LEONIDO: Where are you going?

SHEPHERD: Doing shepherd's work.

LEONIDO: What are sheep to you? Or you to sheep even? Leave them. Let them die as they want to.

SHEPHERD: No. As I want.

LEONIDO: Have you called out?

SHEPHERD: It won't hear.

LEONIDO: Not?

SHEPHERD: So I grieve for it.

LEONIDO: You don't look like grief. Give up.

SHEPHERD: It was too costly for me. I am afraid he shall die.

LEONIDO: Who shall die?

SHEPHERD: Why, the sheep.

LEONIDO: Damn your ignorant sheep! What are you? A Moor?

SHEPHERD: I am no Moor.

LEONIDO: You have the look of one. They are the mercenaries of Allah. They are all cut throats, and stall holders with prayers on their lips and all the time graft at their elbow.

SHEPHERD: *You* are dressed as a Moor.

LEONIDO: I was once dressed as a Sicilian. Christian. But neither Sicilian nor Christian meant anything to me. Who are you? Why are you loitering? What do you want? Alms? Go away.

SHEPHERD: I want no alms. But the debt you owe must be recovered.

LEONIDO: Perhaps you are a thief. I am a thief myself and I know the signs of a thief. Just as I know a liar. Go away, lunatic.

SHEPHERD: In this meagre pouch is what you owe me.

LEONIDO: Give it to me. I'll look at it. But let me warn you: if you are making game of me, I shall kill you.

SHEPHERD: I hear you.

(*Hands him the pouch.*)

LEONIDO: I can hardly hold it.

SHEPHERD: It is harder still to carry.

LEONIDO: Ah, a conjurer's bag. I knew you had a look of the bazaar about you. Let's look inside. First dip: there's a lucky one. A crown. I shall wear that. It will look better on me. I feel calmer. Emptying this loon's pouch, perhaps. Oh, delightful! A tunic. Oh yes. And with lash marks on it. It looks like a motto, is it your motto, some device? Are the lashes my motto? Why? Do you think

I'm a slave? Like you? What else is there? A rope. That's
good. I may lash you with this. So this is your bond.
What are these things? More clothes.
(*He takes out a cross.*)
Why are you mocking me? If you were God himself,
you'd get no reprieve from me. I am going to kill you.
(*He falls to the ground.*)

SHEPHERD: Why are you afraid, Leonido? Who are you
thinking of? Your mother? Gerardo? Marcela?

LEONIDO: Marcela!

SHEPHERD: Think of your sister's body. Then look into
my heart. Think of your father's eyes. Then look into
mine. Tell me, Leonido, what are you waiting for? What?
Now that the debt is due, what are you thinking of
paying with? Today, Leonido, I have to collect
everything you have spent. I paid for all of them, but
this is the reckoning. And I am here for it.

LEONIDO: I am overspent. It's not in your interest to
believe me. But it is the case. I always knew it would be
so. You will get, if you are so fortunate, a bankrupt's
farewell, which is somewhat less than a penny in the
pound. So be it then. You will have had access to my
books, so there is nothing for me to do but acknowledge
each item, which might give satisfaction to you as a kind
of divine lawyer's fee, but as wearisome to me as the hell
I go to and the hell I came from. You shall have my life,
which is what you came for. It's no more than fluff at the
bottom of the pocket. (*Gives him fluff.*)

SHEPHERD: Let me embrace you.

LEONIDO: Kill me first.
(*The SHEPHERD goes.*)
I'll go to such extremes the world will use me as an
example. Let's off, first with the scimitar. Cloak, hood.
And turban. Tunic, yes, better than the Moorish for a
debtor of my proportions. It's a good garment to stand
trial in. We don't expect acquittal do we? Perhaps *they* do
though. He looked uncertain. No, we want a harsh
tribunal and the full exercise of justice. You, crown, you

sit between my ears, like a child above the crowd. Tears
from ears, tears from the heart, there's a wad of tears.
And rope, rope, you shall need me too. If I'm to settle
up. Be made to seem to settle up.
(*Moves off. Blackout.*
Lights up. Enter ZULEMA and the KING.)

KING: Know this, Zulema. Do not be surprised at Leonido's
reversal. A bad Christian was never a good Moor. When
he followed his own heavenly father, he never kept his
limits. Tunis was no different to him. The man who jeers
at his three-for-one in God will gob in Mahomet's eye
for sixpence.

ZULEMA: There he is. What's he doing?

KING: Kneeling. Go on bind him.

ZULEMA: I will try.

LEONIDO: Come, Moor, come all of you. Leonido is no
longer the same man, but he will flog you a little like he
did before. And then you shall have me. You shall have
your man, defeated as I am. The liar you found so
difficult will become a dismal lamb.
(*They fight. Brutally. Then LEONIDO throws in his hand.*)
Now you may take me.

ZULEMA: It's a trick.

LEONIDO: No more than all the rest, Zulema. Come
along, take this rope around my neck. Grab it, go on. I
am a mule now. Or lamb or what you want of me. If you
want pickings from Mahomet, here's one for you.

KING: Leave him to me, Zulema. *I* want the slaughtering of
this butcher.
(*Chase. LEONIDO laughs. Dances.*)
Got him! Got! You!
(*They bind him with the rope.*)
Let's go. To Tunis.

LEONIDO: To Tunis. Christ support me!
(*Blackout.*
Lights up. LIDORA and TIZON.)

LIDORA: Go on! You are so lethargic. I want to catch up.

TIZON: Yes, ah, the articles, well, you know those already.

LIDORA: And our Father and the Credo.

TIZON: The Ave Mafia.

LIDORA: Go on! Go on!

TIZON: Listen then, Senora I will teach you the precepts which we must observe if we are to enjoy God's favour.

LIDORA: How many are there?

TIZON: No more than ten.

LIDORA: Do you mean a Christian's salvation depends only on ten commandments?

TIZON: That's all.

LIDORA: Tell me what they are quickly. It seems a bargain. But first tell me again how he died. I am confused here. How can man be mortal and immortal at once? How can he die and yet have eternal life?

TIZON: You have grasped the spike of it. Listen: For the first sin which Adam committed against God, for eating the fruit of the world, we are all of us condemned without hope or remedy. Now, because this was a sin against immense God, immense, you see, only another immense being could atone for it. Being God, as he was immortally powerful, like his Father in heaven, he could not die. Could not.

LIDORA: Most interesting. And the next?

TIZON: The next? Well: so he took on the form of a human. Human form, you see.

LIDORA: Yes, I see.

TIZON: And then, being born of a virgin, he was better than any man. Naturally.

LIDORA: I see that.

TIZON: That is the Virgin Mary, well known where I come from, for the comfort of the afflicted, refuge of sinners and so on and so forth and what have you. She gave birth, you see, to this little fellow, in a most unsalubrious sort of place, and, well, there it is, in the end he was crucified and suffered as you heard in the Credo. Is that all?

LIDORA: Tell me, Tizon: shall *I* be able to see God?

TIZON: That's a difficult question as you'd appreciate, madam. No, I would say no. You are of mortal flesh and therefore I don't see how you could be expected to. None of us do. Do you have any wine? This talk makes me –
(*Enter GERARDO, DIONISIO and MARCELA.*)

MARCELA: Lidora! Lidora, my beloved husband. My husband Dionisio is back here among us!

LIDORA: Dionisio! Marcela, how is this?

DIONISIO: One day, Lidora, when your Tunisian troops came to Alicarte, God must have either wanted me to suffer or to be able to see you. My wife, her father, a servant and myself were walking by the shore when the Moors found us. They took the others and left me for dead in the sand. They took my wife from me and this old man, the most respected head in Alicarte. But it was heaven's wish, beautiful Moor, that I should recover, as you can see. Recover to find my father without sight and my wife all but blinded by what she has seen, what no one should see. It is a wicked reunion, I tell you, Moor.

LIDORA: I can think of nothing to say to comfort you. Tizon? I am sure God does not wish Gerardo to see what his son does. For if he did, he would die. Have you come to ransom them?

DIONISIO: I have sold all I can to cover it.

LIDORA: If only I could give them to you, Dionisio, but I cannot. It is true I became their mistress and they serve me but I myself am subject to the King. I am helpless.

GERARDO: It is not my wish to leave you, Lidora. I would rather stay than leave you. In you, Marcela has a sister, a true sister.
(*Enter the KING and ZULEMA, dragging LEONIDO by a rope.*)

MARCELA: Now we are reunited. Take care, Dionisio. I have never looked on this man without some loss to myself or others.

ZARRABULLI: See! A slave!

LEONIDO: I have a debt to pay. Father, sister. Oh, and you, Dionisio. The runt has survived. And Tizon awake at this hour? And Lidora picking up Christian crumbs and comfort from the servants' table?

KING: Lidora, I have done what you asked for. He's brought in. I did it, only to please you. He's about to die. Or, if you say so, not about to die.

LIDORA: He is your prisoner. Just as I am yours.

LEONIDO: Father, I am at your feet, can you feel me? At your feet. Can you hear me call you father? You wished it once. Before I die, Father, note this, note I am your son.

GERARDO: Son.

LEONIDO: By my mother, naturally. And naturally raped, raped was the word I said, by you. As I raped her in her turn. These are uneasy times. Is that not what you would say, Father? We live in troubled times, an age without faith, the young go their sweet wild et cetera ways. You cannot understand? Well, then: ah, mother. She was pregnant. It was beyond *your* doing. You were born old, like Dionisio here. If Marcela drops another of us it will be mine. My daughter. You see. I will explain. It's simple enough before the bond's honoured. We shall get there. Oh: first, she gave birth to a little girl who was carried off in the jaws of a she-bear. Ask me not how, but it is true. I wanted to go after them but I didn't. My mother was crying out. I left the she-bear and went back to her and found there – Marcela. New born and on the rock. Our daughter. My sister.

(*MARCELA collapses.*)

Mark this. Marcela!

GERARDO: No – no more!

LEONIDO: It is quite enough. I am telling you so that you may know what you have to ask pardon for. For, oh yes, then I stabbed our wife, our mother. You see. That, Father, is what happened. Your tiny heart will not deny me absolution?

KING: Zarrabulli! Take him where I told you.

LEONIDO: Lidora: I entrust all my family to you. You will be busy. But you'll not mind. Remember me a little longer.

(*ZARRABULLI drags him out.*)

MARCELA: Where has he gone?

KING: You will soon know, Lidora, I have given him to
you. Now, keep your word.

LIDORA: Very well, King. I am yours.

(*The KING goes to take LIDORA in his arms.*)

ZULEMA: Wait, Berlebeyo, before you do this, listen to me.
Before he died, your father the King gave me this paper.
I was to entrust it to no one and I have not. You must
read it before you are betrothed.

KING: Read it.

(*ZULEMA opens the charter.*)

ZULEMA: It is in his father's own hand, Lidora. It reads,
'Son, I hear of your wanting Lidora. I must tell you she
is not your equal. When I was hunting Christians some
sixteen years ago on the shores of Alicarte in Sicily, I
rescued her from the mouth of a she-bear. She is a
Christian and no match for my son. If you should marry
her, our great Prophet Mahomet will rage against you.
May Allah preserve you. Your father, Amete, Sultan.'

KING: What? Oh, Divine Allah!

GERARDO: Divine heaven!

TIZON: If there's a Pope in Tunis he'll give him
dispensation.

GERARDO: Quiet, fool! Lidora, you are really my
daughter. This story tallies too well with Leonido's.

TIZON: Or well enough.

LIDORA: Oh, Gerardo. I have never known a father; it is
better than the Kingdom of Tunis.

MARCELA: My dearest!

KING: Damn *all* fathers! Well, I am still King of Tunis.
Tizon, bring Leonido here. If it is not too late. I think
you should all be set free. And, well, persuaded to live
together. It should be instructive.

(*Enter ZARRABULLI.*)

ZARRABULLI: Oh, King, it is Argolan! See!

(*LEONIDO hangs from a tree.*)

LEONIDO: All of you... King, famous King. For you pay
me like a king.

MARCELA: Leonido.

LEONIDO: Little sister.

GERARDO: My son.

LEONIDO: Bless you. Old toad!

GERARDO: Tizon, lead me to his body, My sight is returning.

LEONIDO: Give him his sight. Tizon? Too drowsy?
(*TIZON stabs him.*)
Ah! If there is remembrance – I shall remember you.

LIDORA: Berlebeyo, if you will let us, we will take this body with us.

KING: Take it. Go. Bloody Christians, all of you. Go. Back to Alicarte and your blood and Sicily. Help them take him.
(*ZARRABULLI and TIZON take up LEONIDO.*)

TIZON: Well, King, he played a good tune on vituperation. It may not be a bond honoured, but it's a tune of sorts to end with.
(*They drag him off.*)

Curtain.

THE LABYRINTH OF DESIRE

Characters

FLORELA, a lady from Mantua

RICARDO, a courtier at Mantua

ALEXANDER, Duke of Mantua

LEONICIO, servant to Alexander

MARIO, servant to Alexander

CAMACHO, a Spaniard

LAURA, daughter of the Duke of Ferrara

FINEA, Laura's lady in waiting

PARIS, Prince of Urbino

ESTACIO, Paris's servant

The DUKE of Ferrara

CLARINDO, a courtier at Ferrara

The INFANTE of Aragón

MARINO, a page

MENDOZA, a page

MAID

SILVANA, Laura's maid

LIRANO, servant of the Duke of Ferrara

SERVANT

GUARDS

This translation of *The Labyrinth of Desire* was first performed as a staged reading by Theatre Metropolis at the Rose and Crown, Hampton Wick, on 15 May 2001, with the following cast:

FLORELA, Amy Oliver

LAURA, Charlotte Palmer

CAMACHO, Blair Plant

ALEXANDER / MARINO, Michael Yale

PARIS / MARIO, Adam DeVille

FINEA, Laura Sydanie

INFANTE / ESTACIO, Simon Purse

DUKE / LEONICIO, Andrew Fetters

RICARDO / MENDOZA / CLARINDO / LIRANO, Oliver Grills

Director, Jill Downing

Music arranged by Joe Evans

ACT ONE

Enter FLORELA, a lady, and RICARDO.

RICARDO: I am telling you the truth.
FLORELA: And I cannot take it,
    he's tricked me of my virtue.
    All I can do now is to
    turn my sorrow into a sword
    and plunge it deep inside me.
RICARDO: So you think that's the answer?
FLORELA: Well, what better way is there
    to cure my sorrow than to kill myself?
RICARDO: I do not know what to say.
FLORELA: There's nothing that can be said.
RICARDO: Can't you try and forget him?
FLORELA: The heavens would not want me to.
RICARDO: What do you mean?
FLORELA: I think you can guess.
RICARDO: I can hardly believe it.
    I had never suspected from Alexander
    that your affair had gone so far.
    It's unforgivable he should
    want to marry someone else.
FLORELA: His virtuous reputation makes
    his behaviour all the worse:
    He promised me a thousand times
    that he would be my husband.
RICARDO: Passion makes men say many things.
FLORELA: I have only myself to blame.
    I should never have believed him.
RICARDO: There are few men who keep their promises
    once they have satisfied their desires.
FLORELA: Is there any way I can stop him wanting to
    marry?
RICARDO: How could there be?
    If only his new quest were
    motivated simply by love,
    then matters would be easier.

But a desire to become a duke
has also driven him to Ferrara.
The present Duke is very old,
and does not want to die
before his daughter Laura
has found herself a husband.

FLORELA: Are you telling me that Alexander
has gone there just to court a title?

RICARDO: That's what the gossip is.

FLORELA: At least this Ferrarese
woman is beautiful and witty,
or so I have heard.

RICARDO: I hate to tell you this,
but everyone sings her praises.

FLORELA: And what about her brain?

RICARDO: She hasn't got your special intellect,
nor is she a woman of letters, like you.
However, her intelligence is not in doubt.
But why do you want to know all this?

FLORELA: I've got to go and see her.

RICARDO: And whatever for?

FLORELA: I'm just curious to meet
a woman of such wit and beauty.

RICARDO: This is jealousy pure and simple;
you only want to stir things up.

FLORELA: Well, I don't intend simply
to redeem my honour.

RICARDO: This will all end badly,
I am sure of it.

FLORELA: I am afraid she will fall in love with him;
Alexander is a man of persuasive charm.

RICARDO: But do you really think that
she will single him out
among all her many suitors?

FLORELA: Let's stop this conversation.
You have little idea
of what I have in mind,
that's why you're so doubtful.

Oh Ricardo, all I'm asking now
is that you should help me.
RICARDO: Of course I shall,
on condition you stay here.
FLORELA: But if Alexander is going off to
try and inherit Ferrara,
what else can I do?
RICARDO: Fall out of love.
As heaven is on your side,
heaven will find a way to console you.
In any case, you, who have studied so much
that people call you the Mantuan Sybil,
you, whose wisdom outshines
that of the greatest of intellects,
and whose fame as a poet,
mathematician and philosopher
has been endlessly celebrated,
will surely discover within yourself
a means of consolation and distraction.
FLORELA: What I have learnt from books
might help me stop loving him.
But for my lost honour,
I can see little other solution
than to go and prevent his marriage.
RICARDO: And what if he found you in Ferrara?
FLORELA: That does not frighten me at all:
my studies have taught me
not to be afraid even of dying;
learning has respect only for honour.
RICARDO: That's all very well,
but if honour means so much to you,
you will only lose it by leaving Mantua,
for to do so would be tantamount
to a public announcement of your misfortune,
and letting the whole town know what you are up to.
FLORELA: There's nothing you can say
that will stop me from carrying out my plan:
whether I'm left with honour or without it

I have to prevent him from marrying;
and if dishonour follows on from dishonour,
how can I suffer more than I am?
I shall just have to tell everyone
I'm making a pilgrimage to Loreto
in fulfilment of a vow.

RICARDO: I promise to keep your secret.

FLORELA: Honour was never lost
while its loss was kept secret.
Leave me now, for I must
prepare for my departure.

RICARDO: I'm going, and may the heavens console you

FLORELA: I am praying to them for a cure.

RICARDO: The mind will find one,
especially such a mind as yours.
(*Exits.*)

FLORELA: My firm heart was conquered by Alexander;
no woman's heart is firm enough against first love;
the citadel that protected it has been breached
and all that was virtuous within lies tarnished.
The high wall of my honour, so finely tooled
with precious ornament, has fallen to the ground,
and the governor of the citadel has lifted up
the drawbridge so that love can no longer enter.
Nature, in helping women to listen and understand,
has enhanced with wax the greatest of the senses –
that of hearing. Oh women, if love should try and conquer,
what use is it to have a heart as firm as diamond
when the gateway to the ears is fashioned out of wax?
(*Exits.*
Enter ALEXANDER and his servant LEONICIO.)

ALEXANDER: Are we ready to set off?

LEONICIO: Whenever you want to.

ALEXANDER: Let's leave as secretly as possible.
Though we go under cover of darkness,
it is better that we were not seen at all.

LEONICIO: A person in love is as sharp-sighted as a lynx,
you will never be able to hide from her.

Remember Ovid's tale of the abandoned Clicia,
who became a sunflower so as to keep
a constant eye on her faithless lover in the sky:
wherever you go, Florela too will be looking at you.
ALEXANDER: My only wish is that she does not chase
me beyond the confines of this town.
I am not bored with Florela,
I still love her as I love myself;
the guilty party is Opportunity,
who, in offering me a chance to marry,
has forced me to choose between
two women of a very different kind.
One of them, though my equal in nobility,
has such a clever turn of mind that she
makes me feel as coarse and simple as
an oak in the face of a triumphal palm.
The other is the resplendent Laura,
who, if her reputation is anything to go by,
restores to this modern age
the shining beauty of ancient times.
Need I add that the person who marries her,
will become the next Duke of Ferrara?
LEONICIO: In love you should always be guided
by your instinct and never by ambition.
ALEXANDER: As I see it my greatest obligation
in this case is to personal gain.
Let Florela cry if she has to,
let her plead to her heart's content,
let her be a flower chasing the sun,
but the sun, I'm afraid, is soaring high,
and disappearing off into another world,
leaving Clicia hidden in a dark Antarctic sea.
LEONICIO: I can only pity her tears
once she has been banished
to the shadows
by the rays of your glory.
(*Enter MARIO, another servant.*)
MARIO: Someone else from Ferrara has come to see you.

ALEXANDER: Is he another messenger from my friend
                                        Clarindo,
    reporting back on the latest news from Laura?
MARIO: I have no idea, sire, why he is here.
    If you let him in, I'm sure he'll tell you.
ALEXANDER: But what sort of person is he?
MARIO: It's difficult to tell.
    He has the tall boots and uniform of a page,
    but he's unlike anyone else I've seen at court.
ALEXANDER: Tell him he is welcome,
    and show him in.
MARIO: Enter, dear sir.
    (*Enter CAMACHO, in an exhausted state.*)
CAMACHO: Your Excellency, I know exactly what you're
                                        thinking.
    You were expecting a court emissary
    to be a man of stature and stoic dignity,
    and not the sweaty mass of aching bones
    you see before you.
    I have been in such a rush to
    deliver this letter from Clarindo that I no longer
    know whether I'm coming or going.
ALEXANDER: You'll be able to rest shortly.
    I swear that if you had delayed another minute
    you wouldn't have found me here.
    Let me read what you've brought.
LEONICIO: I've never known a messenger like him!
MARIO: He's quite extraordinary!
CAMACHO: I'm happy to serve any master,
    as long as I can do so sitting comfortably;
    for has ever a knight suffered so much in his
    travels as has of late my poor old bum?
    The other parts of the body will probably all
    agree that bums deserve at times a good old shaking
    for being so coarse, lazy, and downright cheeky.
    The eyes and the ears have every right to complain,
    for they don't just hang around doing nothing,
    but are busy all the time guiding us like lanterns,

or listening to crap. The tongue as well is actively
employed, even though some prefer it when not used at all.
Feet are worked off their feet, and hands do all the handling;
in short only the bum can happily spend its day
just sitting on its arse, sleeping even when it's off the
                                                    ground,
and getting fat from lack of work, and sybaritic living.
So thank you, Jupiter, the other body parts will say,
for inventing the mail coach so that the bum can suffer
in a single day more than it has in all its years of doing fall.

ALEXANDER: I have now read Clarindo's letter,
and am frankly amazed that
a man of my standing has so many
competitors for Laura's hand.

CAMACHO: Well, what's so surprising?
Laura is very beautiful,
the Duke's on his last legs.
No wonder that the whole
of Italy wants to win her love
I can't tell you how many
noble Princes I've left
prancing about in Ferrara,
preening themselves in finery
you've never seen the like of,
flirting outrageously,
and organising such dazzling
balls, parades, tournaments, and the like
that the sun will soon be calling it a day,
unable to compete with so much brilliance.
Sadly, I have not the wit to do full justice
to all the wonders I have seen;
in this pretentious age of ours
you need too many fancy words
to praise without offending.
Under normal circumstances,
I wouldn't mind having a go, say,
at describing the Duke of Urbino's horses –
I'm a foreigner after all,

and the main reason we leave our countries
is so that everyone can criticise us, and take the piss.
However, given the memory lapses
occasioned by the arduous journey in getting here,
not to mention the current state of my bum,
all I can say about the magnificent horses
that everyone was raving about
is that they walked around on four legs.

ALEXANDER: There is no need to say anything more,
and add to my present worries.
In any case, even if the Duke's horses
were as marvellous as you say they are,
I am sure that as soon as I arrive myself at
Ferrara, people will begin to wonder
what they ever saw in that upstart from Urbino.

CAMACHO: Have you got a lot of money on you?

ALEXANDER: Yes I do.

CAMACHO: Well, you can count yourself a certain winner
then:
in the court circles of today,
nothing impresses so much
as a prince who's generous with his money.
You'll have the world in your pocket,
and even clerks will bless you for it.

ALEXANDER: And what about my royal parentage?

CAMACHO: That's not so important.
Extravagant gestures are what matter now.
Make sure to boast of your wealth
to the silversmith, the merchant,
and any one else whom you might employ
down to the humblest shoemaker.
Then everything else will follow.
You will find yourself praised in all the arts,
poets will become rich making
the world hear of all your hidden virtues,
painters will be known for celebrating your
features in a thousand glorious portraits;
and even lawyers will be beneficiaries,
as they twin their names with yours,

acting in your defence, or fighting you in court.
The end result is that everywhere you go there'll
be people saying, 'Look, there's that man from Mantua.'
And if, after all this, you've still got money left,
keep on being generous into your dotage.
Make sure to pay your doctors well,
and cures for gout and other maladies will suddenly be
                                                    found;

and when these all fail, all you need to do
is to become a donor to the Church,
and then you'll have the consolation
of ending your life in style, with funeral celebrations
that will ensure your glory for at least
two thousand years to come, Amen.
ALEXANDER: Your sense of humour
and your way of speaking,
have made me curious.
Who are you,
and where are you from?
CAMACHO: My fatherland is Spain, sir,
and I am currently a page to Clarindo,
who offered to help me out for a while after
I had turned up from Bologna University,
rather ill-qualified, I have to confess.
I could have stayed on there to take my degree
and wear a doctor's gown and board;
but the university these days has so many hangers-on
that I would have ended up dying of hunger.
ALEXANDER: Would you like to serve me instead?
CAMACHO: Nothing in the world would please me more,
and Clarindo, I'm sure, will be pleased as well,
to see the back of me.
ALEXANDER: Alright then, that is settled.
I hope you're ready to depart,
I cannot afford to lose another minute.
CAMACHO: Don't worry about my rest,
I'll happily do without it
knowing that in following you
I march towards stability and security.

ALEXANDER: You'll soon forget your tiredness.
CAMACHO: Look, all my aches and pains have gone
already.
ALEXANDER: Let's be going then.
　And if Florela comes here after me in hot pursuit
　let her be told to look for me in Laura's arms.
　(*Exit.*
　Enter LAURA and her lady-in-waiting FINEA.)
LAURA: No-one's ever going to please me.
FINEA: I cannot understand why ever not.
LAURA: But I can, Finea, only too well.
　It's just that I don't know how to put it.
FINEA: You are not normally so shy.
LAURA: No, but being as now the object of
　so much male attention is making me
　retreat into myself and wish almost
　I was a woman forgotten by the world.
　I must confess as well that I find it difficult
　to be drawn to anyone who tries to court me
　without having love as their final goal.
　All that really interests my many suitors
　is the prospect of the Dukedom of Ferrara;
　They desire me only for their own ambitions.
FINEA: You must try and be more reasonable.
　Instead of thinking in the abstract
　about your choice of husband,
　you should let your thoughts
　be governed more by your desires,
　so that your thoughts become more pleasing.
　Of course, it's true that love alone
　is not your suitors' only interest.
　However, contrary to what you think,
　it is not your lands but your beauty
　that will make the final conquest.
　Oh, out of interest, what do you
　think of this Urbino man
　that everyone is always talking about?
LAURA: He is in every respect the perfect gentleman.

FINEA: Everyone is counting on him to win your heart.

LAURA: Well, I am sorry, I'm not yet inclined to give it to
him.

Every time I see someone who takes my fancy,
I end up suffering a thousand irritations,
because whenever I look into the person's eyes
all I can see are the estates of my father;
and as these include numerous towns,
I feel my chest is just not big enough
to accommodate so many battlements.

FINEA: I suspect your heart is less rigid than you think,
and that one day love will breach its gates.
That it has not done so yet does indeed suggest
that it is power and not a woman that your suitors seek.

LAURA: You are absolutely right. What do I care
if all the greatest and most presentable men in Italy
are crowding at my gates if not a single one of them
has any interest in what's inside a woman's soul?
I insist that I, Laura, am the loved one
and not the Dukedom of Ferrara,
for what value is there in living
if one's own life is not appreciated?
(*Enter a MAID.*)

MAID: There's foreign woman at the door, my lady.
She's passing through Ferrara on her way to Loreto,
and has heard so much about you and your beauty
that she wishes to see you for herself, and get acquainted.

FINEA: Well, there you are, you already have an admirer
who values you for your own qualities.

LAURA: I am happy to hear it. Tell her I shall be delighted
to see her.

(*Enter FLORELA accompanied by MAIDS.*)

FLORELA: Your Excellency, give me your hand.

LAURA: If I was the sun I would give you all my rays,
and concede defeat to one whose eyes
shine with a divine and incomparable radiance.

FLORELA: Please, stop there, otherwise I shall have no
other choice
but to draw a curtain before the sun, and shield my eyes.

You weaken me so much from shame and awe
that I risk being blinded instantly by your brilliance,
and shall have to go away without claiming to have seen
you.
It is said of Phaeton that a strange and powerful urge
made him dare one day to climb up to the palace of the sun.
He saw crystal columns set on emerald bases,
and gilded vaults, and wreaths of coral and marble.
And he saw a topaz throne, and on it sat the sun,
as wonderful and mesmerising as a golden flower.
The sun lent him its chariot, and he drove around the skies,
but though he tried his best and was unguided by self glory,
he could not master the chariot's horses, who, sensing his
confusion,
hurtled out of orbit, and threatened universal conflagration,
until finally he was struck by fire and thrown into the sea,
where, blinded and burnt, he met a cold and soothing end
(if only others so enflamed could have the luck to fall in
water).
Well, here before you is a woman who is tempting
Phaeton's fate,
and who has been driven by tales of your rare beauty
to climb up to your palace and see you in your robes of
flame.
Moderate, I implore you, the brightness of your light,
and know how strong the power is that lies in your control.
If not, my gross temerity shall have me falling through
the skies until
my scorched body is drowned in the sea of my profound
unworthiness.
LAURA: You seem a person of such learning and exquisite
turn of mind
that you will surely understand how I, as your imagined
sun,
can only be disturbed at seeing the laurels that are your
crown.
You will remember, I hope, the tale of haughty Daphne,
who, fleeing like the wind from the sun's heated passion,

and fearful of being caught, turned for help to her father
                                                    Peneus.
She was turned into a laurel tree, and her leaves were placed
upon the sun's repentant head in memory of this cruel story.
It would thus be best to think no more of suns and laurels,
unless, of course, you are happy resting quietly on my
                                                    forehead.
I can assure you that, in contrast to what I have just related,
the thought of you there does not serve to prick a guilty
                                                    conscience
but makes me instead feel proud, confident and glorious.
FLORELA: I see now that all the wonders I have heard tell
                                        of you are true,
    you enrich nature with both your beauty and your mind.
    But, surely you must be wondering now who I am.
LAURA: I admit I was beginning to feel a little curious.
FLORELA: There's nothing much to tell.
    I am not a noblewoman of your standing,
    but I am noble in my heart,
    and, though drawn here
    by a fascination with your fame,
    I would be happy now
    to serve you, if you wish.
    I promise that if you were
    to grant me this request
    I would only work for you
    and no-one else.
LAURA: Have you any other ties at present?
FLORELA: If I did, I certainly would not
    offer you my services so freely.
LAURA: Where are you from?
FLORELA: I am from Rome.
LAURA: And what's your name?
FLORELA: Diana.
LAURA: I would love you to stay,
    but not just as part of my retinue.
    I want us to share equally
    my duties and my burdens.

FLORELA: I do not know how I can thank you
    for such kindness.
    All I can I say is that I hope
    you shall soon have the chance
    to know my special gifts.
LAURA: Your sharpness of mind
    is what will serve me best.
FLORELA: As a secretary I think you
    will find me extremely useful.
    I have a ready tongue,
    and know all the main languages.
LAURA: I cannot tell you how much
    your arrival here has brought
    me new cause for hope and joy.
    Your timing is quite perfect,
    for I need now more than ever
    good advice and a fluent pen.
    I am not sure if you have heard
    about my father's campaign
    to try and have me married,
    and how, with this lofty aim in mind,
    he has invited to Ferrara
    the finest princes in the land.
    With this achieved, he has done his part;
    now all depends on me, and how I chose between
    these many suitors, all of whom have
    few apparent scruples in telling me or
    writing down in letters every little
    thought that comes into their heads.
    This is where I am counting on you,
    and on your wisdom and discretion
    to help me sort through this maze of ardour,
    so that I can finally marry,
    in fulfilment of God's and my father's will.
FLORELA: You do me, my lady, the greatest of honours;
    but I really think that in this case
    your faith in me will be fully rewarded.
    I am already aware of the reasons for your marriage

and know some of the men involved.
It is clearly vital for someone of great learning,
to act as your adviser.
Without wishing to boast unduly,
I should inform you that I have won my laurels
in all the main branches of the arts and sciences.
LAURA: I am certainly hoping to turn to you
    when it comes to testing out my suitors.
FLORELA: What do you mean?
LAURA: I shall need a place of cool repose
    from which to escape at times
    from so many shining reputations
    and heated displays of love.
FLORELA: Laura, not one of these men
    shines in the way you do;
    in any case, it is their actions
    that matter, not their words or reputation.
FINEA: Come and take a look through this window.
    There they all are, showing off their manliness.
    I cannot believe that love is not to be found
    amidst so much youth and beauty.
LAURA: That's for Diana to decide;
    I leave myself entirely in her hands.
FLORELA: Perhaps you can show me yourself
    how you like a man to behave.
LAURA: From now on, fair Diana,
    your wishes are my wishes.
FLORELA: I want the sun of your virtue
    to cast its light on me.
LAURA: And I ask the same of you,
    for in your heavenly realm,
    I have already found new life.
FLORELA: (*Aside.*) Oh proud Alexander,
    I shall come back down again to earth,
    before I let you marry Laura!
    (*Exit.*
    Enter PARIS (*the Duke of Urbino's son*) *and his servant*
    ESTACIO.)

PARIS: Has that Mantuan man arrived yet?

ESTACIO: He certainly has, I've never known
a man of such commanding presence.
His size and stature make the ladies blink.

PARIS: I want more details.

ESTACIO: Well, he's young and handsome,
has a black beard, and is somewhat swarthy.

PARIS: A lot of finery?

ESTACIO: He has not shown it yet.
His parade is not scheduled until tomorrow.

PARIS: And his travel clothes?
Were they of plain fabric, or fancily embroidered?

ESTACIO: Blue linen shirts embroidered with gold and red
thread;
jackets of the purest white,
and hats studded with diamonds.

PARIS: Alright, he's rich. But don't think
I'm going to lose any sleep over this.
His wealth might impress the Duke, but
it's Laura who has to make the choice,
and she does not rush into decisions.
I do admit, though, his imposing size
is rather worrying.

ESTACIO: Don Juan, the Infante of Aragón, is also here,
you should look out for him as well.
He's the one who was born and bred in Naples.

PARIS: Don't tell me he's yet another suitor?

ESTACIO: I'm afraid he is; he's come because he has no chance
of succeeding from his father, even if his brothers die.

PARIS: My hopes seem ever vainer by the moment.
There's no end to my rivals, Estacio!

ESTACIO: So many have been pouring in these days
that the whole palace is looking like a giant waiting-room.

PARIS: And how did the Infante make his processional entry?

ESTACIO: With one hundred of the finest Spanish stallions.

PARIS: I can see them all before me.

ESTACIO: And what a sight it was!
The horses, striped with the ancient arms of Aragón

advanced like a shimmering velvet sea of reds and yellows,
while their heads, crowned with plumage from the East
fantastically adorned with silk and silver trimmings,
moved in unison with such rhythm and precision
that each neigh seemed like a gesture of command,
prompted by riders who showed a skill that Phaeton
lacked…

PARIS: There is no need to continue, my envy is
sufficiently aroused.
    If only I had had the sense to buy one hundred horses!

ESTACIO: The Duke is coming.

PARIS: Who do you think will be the chosen one?

ESTACIO: The person who least deserves it.
    (*Enter the DUKE of Ferrara, followed by CLARINDO and
    their retinue.*)

DUKE: The more suitors that continue to arrive
    the greater are my worries and my confusion.

PARIS: I kiss your feet, sire.

DUKE: Oh, Paris, how it pleases me to see you!

PARIS: I fear you are unwell, sire.

DUKE: When someone is overcome with sadness,
    who is to say what their state of health is like?
    For those venerable doctors from ancient Athens
    sadness itself was considered a terrible disease,
    greater almost than any other known to Man.

PARIS: The troubles of the soul should indeed be thought
of as an illness,
    for they transmit to the body all their pains and cares,
    and alter so much the constitution of the sufferer,
    that real and serious maladies can at times occur.
    But can you tell me the cause of your unhappiness?

DUKE: I can.

PARIS: You are always doing me, sire, a thousand favours.

DUKE: This seems hardly one of them, for can you not
guess the cause?
    Or do you not think that having so many princes
rushing to Ferrara
    in the hope of marrying my daughter insufficient reason
to be concerned?

PARIS: Why should it be, sire? Surely, having such a
                                  choice of suitors
    means you can find for her the man she truly deserves.
DUKE: Paris, I should make it clear that I do not intend to die
    ill-loved by all the friends I have in Italy.
    Let Laura chose for herself, so that if anyone wishes
    afterwards to complain, she alone can take the blame;
    I leave the matter of her marriage entirely in her hands,
    for she, after all, is the one who has to marry.
PARIS: But what if you don't agree with her choice?
DUKE: Whether I agree or not, she'll be the one to take
                                   responsibility.
PARIS: Everyone else in Italy, though, will think the choice
                                   was yours.
DUKE: (*To CLARINDO.*) What on earth is Laura up to now?
CLARINDO: When I last saw her, she was alone in the garden
    with Diana, her wise secretary from whom
    she is never for a moment parted.
DUKE: I have never seen such love between a pair of
                                   humans,
    it's hardly natural.
CLARINDO: But it's not surprising that my lady should
                                   want to spend
    so much time with a woman of Diana's beauty and
                                   understanding.
    If I were her I too would wish for so wonderful a companion
    to pass my days together amidst fountains and laurel trees,
    reading and writing a thousand heartening verses.
    I have heard it said that in poetry Diana is the equal to
                                   Apollo.
DUKE: Call Laura here this instant.
CLARINDO: I shall, sire.
DUKE: If my daughter is devoting herself all day
    to poetry, reading, and loving Diana,
    how can I be shocked that she is losing
    all feelings common to women of her age,
    and showing so little interest in marrying?

PARIS: There is much talk, sire,
    about this lady whom
    Laura has so tenderly received.
DUKE: You do well to wonder at her reputation; I was so
                                            incredulous
    at first that I became determined to find out if there was
                                            any truth behind it.
    In the end I arranged one day to have her tested in
                                            debate before
    all the learned men from far and wide who are gathered
                                            at my court.
    And do you know what happened? Not only did she
                                            excel herself,
    but she turned out to know far more than all of them
                                            put together.
PARIS: She deserves a crown of gold and laurel.
    (*Enter LAURA.*)
LAURA: What do you want, your Excellency?
DUKE: My darling Laura,
    What are you doing to me, why are you killing me with
                                            your absence?
    You are fleeing me like you would some spurned lover,
    for you must know that there is no-one in this earth who
                                            loves you more than I.
LAURA: Let me kiss your feet; and, let me assure you of
                                            my love
    by saying that I am not just fleeing you but everyone.
DUKE: Well, if only you could prove this love in a different
                                            way.
    All I want from you is to free me of that great worry
    that is hanging over me, so I can die without it.
PARIS: (*Aside.*) Oh, holy Christ!
    It must surely be me whom he wants Laura to marry!
LAURA: Sire, you know I live only to make you happy,
    and that I must respect your every wish.
    Please, tell me, which one of my suitors do you want me
                                            to love?
PARIS: (*Aside.*) Oh God, please put my name between his lips!

DUKE: You know too well that the decision can only be yours;
   I am resolved to accept whoever you might chose.
LAURA: Since my father's real wish is for me to marry the
                              Prince of Urbino,
   perhaps something should be said now that he is here...
   Sire...
DUKE: Come on, speak up then, don't be afraid.
PARIS: (*Aside.*) Oh Lord in heaven, and all the planets in
                              the universe,
   come to my assistance: the stars have ordained that today
   should be a day of suffering for a man too much in love;
   make me now find peace with Laura, even if she needs
   a little forcing. And though you must not force the stars,
   would it be possible at least to make them well disposed?
LAURA: Sire, you have to give me three more days.
DUKE: Three days then I shall give you to end this shameful
                              saga:
   spend the two nights profitably, consulting with your pillow.
   It is unfair to keep so many princes in suspense, with
                              their armies waiting,
   let alone the despairing old man who has looked after
                              you since birth.
   (*Exit all, except LAURA.*)
LAURA: Not even Lisimacus setting out to fight the lion,
   nor Aeneas making his way along the Stygian river,
   nor Hercules doing battle with the hideous monster,
   nor Caesar subjugating France to Roman rule,
   nor Orpheus opening with his lyre the gates of Hell,
   had a challenge equal to that of choosing one's husband.
   The decision of a life-time should not be made too lightly;
   and those who throw themselves unthinkingly into marriage
   should not complain of loss of liberty when all goes badly.
   (*Enter FLORELA.*)
FLORELA: I was so depressed without you
   that I could no longer bear the company of flowers.
LAURA: Your love means such a lot to me.
FLORELA: What are you doing here all on your own?
LAURA: My father is the one to blame,
   he left me here too hurt and stunned to move.

FLORELA: Hurt? Stunned? What did he say?

LAURA: He could not bear my indecision any longer.

FLORELA: But why bother to allow you to chose a husband
    if in the end he forces you to chose one badly?

LAURA: Oh, Diana, how many times did you warn me
    that this day would come!

FLORELA: You worry me more than ever.
    You have suddenly gone deadly pale.
    Where has all the colour gone
    from your radiant cheeks?

LAURA: It's gone to help my heart,
    which is still pounding with the shock.
    I have always been afraid of
    my father's tyrannical temper;
    but it was the urgency of his manner
    that changed my complexion,
    and weakened my resolve.
    So all I asked was three more days
    in which to choose, thus forcing me
    to find a master of my affections
    from among the suitors already here…
    To tell the truth, I tremble at the
    thought of doing so, and of the enemies
    I am bound to make.
    All that helps to calm my nerves
    is the knowledge that with you
    as my adviser, I cannot surely make the
    wrong decision and end up sad and hated.
    Tell me, Diana, who is it to be?
    Should I throw in my lot with the Prince of Urbino?
    Or do you find the Frenchman Leonardo
    a more exciting proposition?
    And what about the Infante of Aragón,
    or that worthy German Balduino?
    Do you want me perhaps to marry Gonzaga,
    or do you think Octavio or Lucindo
    are more suitable recipients of my love?
    Or do you feel that not of these seven men,
    can match that new arrival Alexander?

I was almost conquered by his name alone,
even before I saw the man himself,
parading this morning below my balcony
like some proud hero from ancient times.
I hope I do not shock you if I bluntly say that
his was an ardour that burnt with real heat,
and that I felt transformed like a sunflower
when touched by the brilliant rays from his eyes.
But what has come over you? Why have you gone so sad?
You do not think that just because I am going to marry
our sweet and honest friendship will be all forgotten?
I shall never ever leave you, you know full well.
I shall be with you all day, Diana,
and even at night, I shall think of you as a point of refuge
from which to flee the male enemy that has come between
us.
Are you crying? My God, you really are crying!
You are making me weep as well.
Come on, you poor thing, look straight into my eyes.
You know you do me wrong by even
doubting for a moment what I have told you:
there is nothing that can break our friendship,
not even the demands of a husband.
FLORELA: If only I could tell you, Laura,
if only I could tell you the truth!
Of course I can see why you think
that marriage will do nothing to affect our friendship,
that everything will go on as before
and that you will not stop loving me.
But if only I were able to reveal what
I have so shamefully hidden from you, Diana,
then you would appreciate why
I have no other choice but to kill myself straight away,
and put a final end to all this deception.
LAURA: You are making me all confused and frightened.
What could you possibly be hiding from me?
How can a friendship be a true one if it is not based on
honesty?

Surely, you must realise that you do more harm
by keeping your secret than bringing it out into the open?

FLORELA: Oh God, but who could possibly dare to reveal
such a secret as mine?

LAURA: You know I shall never tell anyone.
Even if you said you were planning to kill my father
I would keep it to myself, and suffer silently.

FLORELA: But I just do not know how to say it.
Please wait a bit, my heart is beating too fast,
I must try and calm my nerves.

LAURA: Just say it, please!

FLORELA: And what if anyone interrupts us?

LAURA: We shall quickly change the conversation.

FLORELA: I am, most generous Laura,
on whom the heavens have always smiled,
and to whom I shall always be unworthy,
I am…but my nerve is failing once again,
how can I possibly say this?
I am a man.

LAURA: Holy Christ!

FLORELA: You see, was not my fear justified?

LAURA: You, a man?

FLORELA: Well, if this upsets you so much, Laura,
I shall go back again to being a woman;
remember, you swore that you would keep my secret.

LAURA: If only I had known what I was swearing to;
you have made me more confused than ever;
but I cannot help thinking that you are just using
your rare and unusual mind to play a trick on me.

FLORELA: I am not tricking you, Laura, I am not.
But it would best not to ask for proof,
for if the truth gets out, the consequences would be fatal.

LAURA: But how can you expect me to accept what you say
if the person before me appears in every way a woman,
down even to her way of walking and behaving?
How can I possibly be silent and not amazed
if what I am hearing does not tally at all with what I am
seeing?

If you suddenly go and tell me that you are a man,
you cannot be surprised if you get some scepticism in
                                                        return.
FLORELA: Lower your voice, Laura, have you forgotten
                                        where we are?
You are not in the middle of a field, or high up on a
                                        mountain,
with only streams and rivers as our witnesses.
You are in your house, Laura, your house;
You are surrounded by relatives, courtiers and servants,
all of whom would not hesitate for a moment to punish
                                        my offence;
But hear me out Laura, listen to the rest of my story;
LAURA: Diana, I do not know what to say to you;
all I know is that transformations of this sort
are only the stuff of ancient fables:
perhaps you have learnt a thing or two from Jupiter,
who took on female form to have his way with
one of the Goddess Diana's innocent maidens;
I need not remind you of the outcome of that story,
the maiden's fate is written nightly in the stars.
FLORELA: There is little point in my being with you,
if you cannot be bothered to listen to me.
LAURA: But what is there to add after such a revelation?
FLORELA: But I would rather you heard it in full;
you will have plenty of time to kill me afterwards.
LAURA: Are you really, really a man?...
I just cannot believe this to be true!
FLORELA: Laura, in seeing you so disbelieving,
I am beginning to suspect that
part of you wanted me to be what I have become.
There was once a man who loved a statue so much
that the gods eventually gave in to his pleas,
and turned the marble into the person he desired.
Well, your love for me has had the same effect.
Why, it was only an hour or so ago,
when you were telling me between the elms
how much you loved me, that you said:

'If only you were a man, I would let you be my only
                                              master.'

And now that you have got your wish,
    and some miracle of love has transformed me into a man,
    why are you so angry, what more do you want?
LAURA: I am not angry.
FLORELA: Well, what's wrong then?
LAURA: I am just concerned, that's all;
    I mean, if the woman whom I valued so highly
    has suddenly become a man
    what is there to stop this person
    becoming a woman again on the wedding night?
FLORELA: My dear Laura, believe me; I am a man.
    While still a male, and barely out of school,
    I was taunted into killing the heir to my country's throne.
    I had six sisters, and the danger I was in forced me
    to disguise myself among them,
    and wear the type of clothes you see me wearing now.
    Thanks to my delicate skin and girl-like features
    you know so well, I went unrecognised by the authorities
    when they searched for me in every corner of the house.
    My parents colluded with this strange deception,
    and acted as if the boy they once had known was dead;
    I let my hair go long and flowing like a maiden's.
    For two years I kept up this female role at home,
    as if I was the fair Achilles, whose mother Thetis
    dressed him as a girl to keep him from the Trojan war.
    There was not a part of Italy where my searchers did not
                                              look,
    unaware that all the time I had never left my town,
    and was living openly in my parent's house.
    I joined the young maidens in the women's quarters,
    helping them with their embroidery and other dainty tasks;
    I even went with them into the baths, and enjoyed unnoticed
    their beautiful naked bodies fooling in the water.
    And when they wondered why I never bathed as well,
    I feigned a modesty that prevented me from publicly
                                              undressing.

But in every other way I was exactly as a woman,
and learnt to emulate so well their every single gesture
that I almost forgot entirely what it was to be a man.
Indeed so seductive was my dress and bearing that
I was soon courted by a gentleman, in whom I began
to see a devious chance to escape my curious fate.
I had to put up with no end of silly letters, nightly serenades
and amorous recitations that are usually only bearable
when you are separated from the person by a wall.
Eventually, however, seeing this as my only way to freedom,
I arranged for him to lead me secretly outside the house.
But no sooner was he with me than he began to behave
        so stupidly
that I had to disillusion him of my femininity by taking
        out my sword.
I wandered later as a woman throughout the whole of Italy,
and was in Venice when I heard about your father's plans.
I saw your portraits, Laura, and found in them such
        grace and beauty
that no prospect seemed more pleasurable than to serve you.
Since then you have put so much trust in me
that I felt it wrong you should think of me as a woman.
But I had not the courage to let you know the truth.
My love has grown along with yours;
I am not alive if I do not see you;
I cannot sleep for thoughts of you,
and when I sleep you are always in my dreams.
Laura, if you say to me now that you are marrying,
you can count me dead, already...
I cannot bear this any more...
LAURA: This is quite extraordinary!
You have succeeded in making me believe you,
I no longer have the heart to say what I was going to.
Please stop your tears, you are making me sad as well.
Although you have committed an offence against my
        father's honour,
the faith and love I have invested in your mental prowess
oblige me for the moment to hold back my punishment,
and perhaps even my marriage.

FLORELA: Give me those fair feet of yours.
LAURA: Please try and restrain yourself.
   You make me uncomfortable now when I look at you,
   we should not be alone together in the same room.
FLORELA: I suspect you shall soon get over these feelings.
LAURA: What is your real name?
FLORELA: I am called Felix.
LAURA: Felix, we must not forget about the three days
   that are left to me. You, who appear to be a
   master of disguise and entanglements,
   must find a way of delaying this whole business,
   and taking away some of my suitors' ardour.
   Because if you do not...
FLORELA: Do not be impatient, Laura, I beg you:
   I have a scheme that will put off your
   wedding for a very long time.
LAURA: How so?
FLORELA: All you have to say, my lady,
   is that faced with so many equally illustrious Princes,
   and unwilling to upset them by some unfair whim,
   you have decided that the only sensible solution
   would be to submit them all to a competition.
   And, as the issue at stake is one of love and peace,
   it would be better that they proved themselves
   not in arms but in letters. Your husband, in conclusion,
   shall be the one who proves himself the best in argument,
   and who succeeds in solving some puzzles of my devising.
LAURA: This is a brilliant idea.
   But we must go now,
   I am sure I heard my father in the corridor.
FLORELA: Just one more thing.
LAURA: What is it?
FLORELA: Are we to remain friends?
LAURA: I am not so sure.
   I cannot as yet describe my feelings,
   but I do not look at you now
   with the same satisfaction as before.
FLORELA: Laura, I completely understand;
   but let us speak more about this at our leisure.

The mind, I hope, will help to solve our problems,
and see us through the labyrinth that is desire.

End of Act One.

ACT TWO

Enter the INFANTE of Aragón and CLARINDO.

INFANTE: This is absolutely preposterous.
    All this should have been sorted out
    with arms rather than with stupid riddles.
    I was born to be a soldier
    not a bloody student or professor.
    What chance is there for me
    against the brains of Mantua and Urbino?
CLARINDO: Why ever not?
INFANTE: Well, do you see me as a regular on Mount
                            Parnassus?
    Though I am not as simple and ignorant as some might
                               think,
    I am more at ease with an iron glove than with a pen.
    In any case Laura too is not doing herself any favours.
    A lady's hand is won in battle, damn it, and not over
    an obscure riddle written out on a precious slip of paper.
    And what on earth is this riddle meant to mean?
    It has three parts, each one of which makes me tremble.
CLARINDO: You have only got a riddle to solve?
INFANTE: Good heavens no, that's not even half of it.
    Then there's the oral examination
    given by her secretary. I mean, what ever next?
CLARINDO: But if she is only a woman, why are you so
                              upset?
INFANTE: Listen, I am the Infante of Aragón, my coat of arms
    is big enough to accommodate six of Laura's.
    I do not deserve to be humiliated by a woman.
    Besides, Diana is not your ordinary little secretary,
    they're saying she's a second Apollo, no less,
    and that she's unequalled too in sciences.
    And they say too that it is thanks to her
    a labyrinth is being built in the palace garden
    as the final hurdle to test out every suitor.
    That really is going too far!

First of all you have to satisfy the Sphinx,
then you have to further prove your mental powers
by confronting a genius in reasoned debate,
and then, when the clouds are finally dispersing,
you are thrown into some fearsome labyrinth
where you must grope around in total darkness
until you reach its heart, where Laura waits.

CLARINDO: Do what Theseus did at Knossos, and get
yourself a thread.

INFANTE: You know what I'm thinking?
That I should save myself the bother of wooing Laura,
and start courting instead my enemy Diana.
Though marrying a secretary might go against my
principles,
Diana's intelligence would certainly come in handy.
I know her fame alone has been sufficient to
win her at least one other suitor from the nobility.

CLARINDO: The woman's qualities are indeed remarkable.
I can tell you things about her
that will certainly help to stimulate your curiosity.
Oh look, Alexander has just entered the room.

INFANTE: You must talk to me about Diana.

CLARINDO: I shall, but...

INFANTE: Get on with it.

CLARINDO: It's better we did so somewhere else.
I suggest you leave the room, and wait for me in the
corridor.

INFANTE: I understand completely, you are very tactful.
Even when talking about the virtues of a woman,
it is wise to do so with discretion.

(*Exit the INFANTE. Enter ALEXANDER and CAMACHO.*)

CAMACHO: This piece of paper you're staring at so
incredulously
has been faithfully copied, let me tell you,
from the original that was pinned to one of the palace's
columns.

ALEXANDER: I can say goodbye now to all my future
prosperity.

CAMACHO: All because of a piece of paper?

CLARINDO: What ever is the matter?

ALEXANDER: Oh, Clarindo, women are as changeable as
the moon!

CLARINDO: Do not give up heart, you are not defeated yet.

ALEXANDER: But do you know what has been written
under Laura's name?

CLARINDO: I do indeed, but still find no reason
why a man of your calibre should be so upset.

ALEXANDER: I put all the blame on that secretary of hers.
They say she is named after the chaste goddess Diana,
but she has caused more trouble than Diana's nymph
Callisto –
the one who was seduced by Jupiter in woman's clothing.
It must be she who has set this riddle worthy of the Sphinx.

CAMACHO: Your Excellency, you are losing your head
over what is in effect a piddle not a riddle.
It shall be a doddle to solve, even with
a knowledge of letters as piddling as mine.
If I fail, then let me lose my own head too.

ALEXANDER: That's a wonderful offer that is.

CLARINDO: Never underestimate the good Camacho,
your Excellency.

CAMACHO: Just because a man doesn't wear the scholar's
funeral gown,
or put a funny flat hat upon his head, or have thick glasses,
that's no reason to ignore him, or take him for an idiot.
Indeed the real fool is often the man with all those trappings,
which sometimes serve to hide true crassness and stupidity.
They're rather like those fancy bits and bobs that people
hold in such esteem when applied lavishly to the horse –
when taken off and laid out afterwards on the ground,
you'll see little else but a pile of mud and soiled leather.
Give me then two days, and if I haven't solved the riddle
by then…

ALEXANDER: And how do you propose setting about it?

CAMACHO: I'll go and chew the cud in the company of
my fellow camels,
and munch on desert cucumbers and the leaves of
baobab trees.

ALEXANDER: Well, let's see what you can do.

CAMACHO: The verses seem rather indifferent, if you ask me;
 they are riddled with a thousand imperfections.
 Their only value is to have been written by a woman.

ALEXANDER: Personally I rather like them.

CAMACHO: Let me read them out aloud:
 'I am, I am not; I love what I love not;
 I delude with disillusion,
 I inspire jealousy, from jealousy I die,
 in my suffering is my cure,
 in dying I hope to live;
 remember me as forgotten,
 I am happy in my unhappiness,
 I go backwards to go forwards,
 where I am nothing I am more,
 and where I am more, I am nothing.'

ALEXANDER: Are you really telling me Camacho
 that you can sort all this out in two days?

CAMACHO: I could do it quicker still, by God,
 for knowing little sometimes has its uses.
 Haven't you noticed how men of letters
 can piss around for days in libraries,
 convinced they'll find an answer in their books?

ALEXANDER: Let's say we solve the riddle as quickly
                                        as you say,
 that still does not absolve us from the argument which
                                        follows.
 And though arguing with a woman should not be
                                        difficult for a man,
 our ordeal will not be over until we enter this labyrinth
 that is being planned in emulation of the one at Knossos,
 where King Minos kept his ferocious bull the Minotaur.
 And even if we had an Ariadne to help us with her thread,
 how are we going to reach Laura in the midst of this
                                        great maze,
 which, even in its half constructed state, is rumoured to be
 so dark and confusing and criss-crossed with alleys
 that if a man should lose himself, he would wander around
 for days before dying slowly of hunger, thirst and exhaustion.

CAMACHO: Did you say your name was Alexander?
　　Well I wonder what he'd make of you, your namesake,
　　you know the one they called 'the Great',
　　who tamed wild horses and conquered half the world.
　　But you're not great at all, you're just pathetic.
　　Look, don't even bother with the labyrinth; when it's
　　　　　　　　　　　　　　　　　　　　　completed
　　I shall go myself, and even though the world be reduced
　　to universal chaos, I swear I shall find your Laura only
　　with the aid of a lantern and a good flagon of wine.
ALEXANDER: You bloody idiot, if they allowed you to take
　　　　　　　　　　　　　　　　　　　　　　in light
　　then anyone could go inside and find her.
CAMACHO: You mean, you've got to search for her in the
　　　　　　　　　　　　　　　　　　　　　　dark?
ALEXANDER: Yes, that's what having no light usually means.
　　Apparently, there will be guards posted at the entrance
　　to check and thoroughly search every person to see if
　　they are taking or hiding anything that
　　will keep them going even for as little as a day.
CAMACHO: Will you listen to me for a moment, will you?
　　If there's no other choice but to wander
　　around this labyrinth in total darkness,
　　then we'll have to have a drastic change of plan.
　　I have an idea.
ALEXANDER: Well, what is it then?
CAMACHO: Am I right in saying that it's Diana
　　who's behind all this?
ALEXANDER: You are indeed.
CAMACHO: Well, then. Use your name to conquer her.
　　It's as simple as that.
ALEXANDER: But how? What tricks known to man
　　could we resort to?
CAMACHO: Love. Love is what throws a woman off her
　　　　　　　　　　　　　　　　　　　　　balance
　　and makes her liable to reveal any secret to a man.
　　Of course, love can have the same effect on either sex:
　　we need only think of what it did to that hunk Samson,

who, after being caressed and flattered by Delilah,
made the great mistake of telling her the secret of his
                                                    strength.
Well, if some Philistine was able to prise that out of him,
can you imagine what you could get out of Diana
if some charming suitor came along promising marriage?
CLARINDO: That idea is not so stupid as it seems.
Women are rarely able to keep a secret.
The only problem is finding the right man.
ALEXANDER: That's very true. He has to be the perfect
                                                    gentleman.
CAMACHO: If you're looking for a gentleman and
                                    someone who's discreet,
then you don't have to look any further. I am he.
ALEXANDER: Are you being serious?
CAMACHO: Of course. All I have to do is to get a costume
and pretend to me a nobleman from the Spanish Court.
As people know little about Spain, and no-one here
knows me from Adam, apart from Clarindo of course,
then I'll be able to court Diana without impediment.
And I have such confidence in my diabolical ingenuity
that I shall hoodwink her out of every secret that we want,
and even take from her her soul should this be necessary.
CLARINDO: Well, do you want to give this madman a chance?
He's a master of illusion, I know this from experience.
ALEXANDER: I'm determined to go ahead with his plan;
but we cannot just give him clothes,
we'll have to provide him with a house as well.
CAMACHO: A house! That's going too far!
All you need do is let me be a guest at yours,
and throw in a footman or two,
and perhaps four or six pages.
My princely needs are modest, as you can see.
ALEXANDER: To think of all those dirty tricks those two
                                                    women
have paid on me, what with their labyrinth and riddles.
I want to pay them back in kind, Clarindo.
Come on, let's go and dress him up,
and provide him with his lackeys.

But what about a name? What's the name
most bandied around at the Court of Spain, Camacho?

CAMACHO: 'Carriages', carriages is what everyone's
                                 always shouting for,
   or 'Coches' as we say in Spain. You can call me 'Don
                                        Coches'.

ALEXANDER: Don't you see, Clarindo, what a madman
                                  we're dealing with.

CAMACHO: I was only joshing.

ALEXANDER: What name, then?

CAMACHO: Don Lucas of Galicia.

ALEXANDER: And your title?

CAMACHO: The Marquis of Mal-Odor.

ALEXANDER: I hope no-one smells a rat.
   Let's go then, today's your day for
   being a Marquis and my guest.

CAMACHO: Oh riddle, Oh riddle! Oh fearful labyrinth!
   Here comes a Marquis with lackeys and all!
   But what on earth does one wear when visiting
   a labyrinth, where the alleys are so narrow
   that one's breeches will be crushed,
   and where it's so damned dark that one might wonder
   why bother about dressing up in the first place?

ALEXANDER: Come on, let the man who loses Laura
   gain a laugh instead!
   (*Exit.*
   Enter FLORELA and LAURA.)

FLORELA: I need to speak to you on your own.

LAURA: Well, if you don't call this being on my own,
   then perhaps I am not the Laura who
   thinks she is seeing and adoring you.

FLORELA: Give me your hand, you pretty-eyed thing,
   and tell me what you see in me.
   How am I to you now?
   What do your senses say?

LAURA: My eyes and my ears could not be happier.

FLORELA: If you have any complaint about my hands,
   allow me to show you what they are capable of.

LAURA: Oh no, take your hands away,
    they are capable of coarse surprises!
FLORELA: You know I always speak to you sincerely.
    Well, there's something else I've got to say.
LAURA: Well, what are you waiting for?
    Do not make me too impatient, Felix.
    Cannot you see how my love for you
    is growing by the minute?
FLORELA: All I want to say is that our love has now
    reached such a point that the time has surely
    come for the ultimate favour to be asked.
    Is it possible that you could be one day my wife?
    Or is such a thought too ridiculously far-fetched?
LAURA: Marriage is a duty that sometimes takes away love's
                                            pleasure.
    Love, when governed by the laws, can be a tyranny,
    and not the tender thing that the two of us now enjoy.
    Let's talk now of something else but love, so that we do
    not burden ourselves with such serious thoughts as these.
FLORELA: You have left me in mid air,
    with my soul anxious and frustrated.
    But, tell me, what do propose to talk about
    that will distract us from our love.
LAURA: The love of a rival, for instance.
FLORELA: Alright then, if it is jealousy you want,
    then jealousy it will have to be.
    You are certainly right in thinking
    that no other subject is more guaranteed
    to take away all thoughts of love than this.
    But, remember that the moment love returns
    it does so with far greater force than ever,
    so that what you might gain one moment
    you lose the next, as if you were moving forwards
    while always taking two steps back.
    And who is this rival whom
    you want to talk about so much?
LAURA: Who? Alexander, of course.
FLORELA: Oh, you cruel and ungrateful wretch!
    You do not deserve my love!

LAURA: What are you saying?

FLORELA: How can you possibly think it will
    be alright to talk about Alexander?

LAURA: And why have you suddenly gone
    from being so gentle to being so fierce?

FLORELA: You women are quite remarkable.
    You are incapable of spending more
    than an hour in the company of someone
    you love without introducing jealousy
    into the conversation, and turning
    pleasurable moments into recriminations.
    What possible good will Alexander do us?
    And as for me, my God, bringing him up
    is like giving me a violent fix of poison.
    Instead of mentioning his name, you might
    as well have thrown my heart straight into the fire,
    and reward all my love with cruelty.

LAURA: Please do not be so angry, my dear Felix;
    my intention was not to provoke you
    but to confide in you as a loved one,
    and ask you what I should do about Alexander,
    who, since yesterday, has been trying hard to
    persuade me to speak to him tonight on the terrace.

FLORELA: That is it, you have really gone too far!
    So you still have doubts about what you are going to do?
    Well don't, there is no need to have them any more.
    Go and speak to Alexander, since you speak so well of him.
    Do not spare a thought for me, I shall not be jealous!
    I knew this would happen, I have known it all along.
    Have I not always said that love is never constant
    between unequals, and that inequality breeds discontent?
    Alexander is your equal, go marry him instead;
    but do not bother again to ask for my opinion,
    for I can no longer fulfil my role as your adviser.
    My jealousy is such that I must try and forget you.
    What a sad little person I was for thinking that
    I could love a woman of your social standing,
    when I am just a man of little means unable now

even to reap the rewards of all the loyalty I have invested.
By tomorrow you shall have moved on elsewhere,
and you shall have carried off my soul as well,
leaving my body wracked with an incurable pain.
How mad I was to throw away my every desire and hope
into a sea as changeable and turbulent as yours!
Speak, disloyal Laura, to your gallant and manly Duke,
and you will see how anger can at times give strength
to all those sorry folk you think of as your unequals.
This strength shall be great enough to kill myself;
and with my death, I shall kill your memory too.
If love is in the blood, then in spilling blood
I shall rid myself of all the love that is inside me.

LAURA: Felix, Felix, my darling Felix!
Look at me, I have gone all silent
because your outburst has filled me with
a thousand strong sensations.
Turn on me your tender eyes once more,
because never are men so beautiful
as when they are fired with jealous rage.
You are making me all heated too!

FLORELA: My life is in your hands.

LAURA: If ever I should speak again about the Duke, I...

FLORELA: Get off me, Laura, get off.
I need to cry all on my own;
and I shall burst if I hold back my tears.
I must leave you now,
and when you join me shortly at the fountains
you shall know then the extent
to which I adore you.

LAURA: Please stay with me,
and help restore our friendship.

FLORELA: Not now.

LAURA: Then I shall see you at the fountains.
But what fountains do you mean?

FLORELA: The fountains, Laura, of my eyes.
If you are truly repentant,
then your heart, like a diligent slave,

will go fetch water from the fountains
that are fed from my jealous tears.
(*Exit FLORELA.*)

LAURA: Was ever a woman more confused in love than me?
What strange spell is this that lifts me out of my misery
only to leave me enamoured of a mystery?
My powers of reasoning seem now merely a delusion,
for how can I love so much in the face of disillusion?
This fair and radiant person whom I so adore
sometimes seems to me a woman, and then a man;
one moment I am cheerful, and the next frustrated.
But surely I do no wrong in loving either him or her,
for the soul, unlike the body, can love any living creature.
(*Enter FINEA.*)

FINEA: I have brought you this piece of paper
which I found floating on a fountain pool;
its message, inscribed in blood-red ink,
is one of the strangest I have ever read:
'Laura was here once without Diana.'

LAURA: Strange things have been happening recently
that have left me so perplexed and out of sorts
that I need to talk to you about them.
Finea, I have a secret which you must promise
on pain of death never to reveal

FINEA: I swear I would rather die a thousand deaths
than ever betray a confidence.

LAURA: I love my secretary Diana more
than if she were a woman.

FINEA: I am glad to hear it;
for loving her in the way you do
would not be possible if
you thought of her as
a member of your sex.
If you allow me to say so,
I have often suspected she was a man.

LAURA: You were very perceptive.
I hope my weakness does not shock you.

FINEA: Why ever should it?
>A man of such beauty and wisdom
>is difficult to resist.

LAURA: Listen, Finea, there is something I want you to do,
>and I hope to God that this will work.
>He claims his name is Felix,
>and the story that he has told me of his life
>is so extraordinary as to be worth
>inscribing in full in the Hall of Fame.
>I believed every detail of this tale,
>but later, seeing him at times so coy and reserved,
>I began to wonder if what he said was true,
>and whether he is not what he says he is.
>The chaste modesty to which I am obliged
>by the nobility of my birth prevents me
>sadly from uncovering this sexual enigma.
>You, however, who have nothing to lose
>in terms either of name or reputation
>can help me by pretending to seduce him.
>And if you prove he is a man, I want to be his wife.

FINEA: Some fine little ploy this is!

LAURA: It is a good one, is it not?

FINEA: But are you not worried about the dangers?

LAURA: But what can go wrong
>if all you are doing is play acting?

FINEA: If you realised Laura how quickly
>acting can become for real,
>then I think you would not let me do this.
>But do not worry, just to please you
>I swear not to forget who I am,
>nor the reason why I am seducing him.
>As soon as I have satisfied myself of his virility,
>I shall withdraw.

LAURA: Well, go off and look for him, Finea;
>I am missing him already.

FINEA: Love never ceases to amaze me!

LAURA: But other than love,
>there is nothing else that the soul desires.
>(*Exit LAURA.*)

FINEA: What could possibly have been in my mind when
agreeing to an undertaking as risky as one involving love?
They say that love at first is like a child, and that when
it grows it plunges, daringly, into the wildest regions,
where it advances like soft flesh upon hot coals.
The leafy branch on which is perched the little bird
that is desire, hides the clip that holds the creature back.
How can I therefore put myself so much at risk
by looking closely at what lies behind the leaves?
To approach a man without the slightest fear or shame
is like playing with the blade of a razor-sharp knife –
a small mistake and you'll end up with your fingers cut.
(*Exit.*
Enter ESTACIO and PARIS.)

PARIS: I am going to tear this riddle up
into a thousand little pieces.

ESTACIO: Don't give up too easily.

PARIS: If this is a fair way of going about things,
then I shall eat my helmet.
Me, having to answer riddles?
Me, having to debate?

ESTACIO: I am sure all this is merely
an excuse to protract the whole affair.
Laura is not ready yet for marriage,
all she wants is to tire you all so much
that you go away and let her
choose a husband at her leisure.

PARIS: I am sickened by these new developments,
all they have done is to increase my fears.
And have you seen this labyrinth that
some are calling an intellectual maze?
Can it really be so complex a construction?

ESTACIO: I do not think a Theseus
is needed to work it out.

PARIS: But I wonder if Laura
plans to be another Ariadne,
and think of some device
to help a favourite find his way.
But, who are those people over there?

ESTACIO: Some new arrivals to the Court,
    if there weren't enough already.
    (*Enter CAMACHO dressed as a knight, preceded by two*
    FOOTMEN, and followed by two pages, MARINO and
    MENDOZA.)

CAMACHO: Is that a group of ladies over there?

MARINO: Yes, it is.

CAMACHO: Have they seen me?

MARINO: Yes, sir.

CAMACHO: Come on, hand me my eye-glass.
    If they are ladies, I better take a closer look at them.

PARIS: I wonder who's the new arrival.

ESTACIO: A man missing an eye, by the look of it.

CAMACHO: Hello there! I wonder what the ladies
    think of me in these parts.

MENDOZA: They never stop singing your praises.

CAMACHO: Is that so, honest to God?

MENDOZA: Yes sir; but they're driving us to distraction
    with all their questions about you.

CAMACHO: Are all the ladies interested in me?

MENDOZA: Every single one.

CAMACHO: Well, what are we waiting for.
    Onwards and upwards!

MARINO: You wouldn't believe the number of
    messages and love notes they want us to deliver.

CAMACHO: Pages...

MENDOZA: Sir...

CAMACHO: Are you saying you're not up to all this?

MARINO: No sir, but these are not the sort of tasks
    worthy of our service.

CAMACHO: And are the women ravishingly beautiful?

MARINO: Some of them are quite attractive, sir.

CAMACHO: Come on, what are we waiting for. Onwards
                          and upwards!

MARINO: There are a couple of toothless Methuselans.
    If I were you, sir, I would trade them in for two of the
                          younger models.

CAMACHO: I imagine it's my gold chains they've really
                         got their eyes on.

MARINO: Not at all, sir, it's only you they're after.

CAMACHO: All they want is my love, honest to God?

MARINO: No lady would dream of asking for anything else.

CAMACHO: What are we waiting for. Onwards and upwards!

ESTACIO: My lord the Prince has sent me here to find out
who is your master.

MARINO: Can you not tell who he is simply by seeing him?
Is not his stature reflected in his appearance?
But if you really want to know the details,
he is Don Lucas of Galicia,
the Marquis of Mal-Odor.

ESTACIO: And why has he come here?

MARINO: To court Laura's secretary Diana,
the one who's more than human.

ESTACIO: I shall go and tell my master.

PARIS: You do not have to tell me, Estacio,
I have heard everything; and what I have heard
has made me hopeful of finding a solution to my problems.

ESTACIO: What do you mean?

PARIS: If Diana comes to love this man
as she would a husband,
then the secrets of the labyrinth will certainly be his;
and if I make friends with him then
he shall surely let me in on what he knows.

ESTACIO: Go and speak to him.

PARIS: I shall do so immediately.
Let me kiss your Lordship's hands.

CAMACHO: Who is this man, Marino?

MARINO: He is the Prince of Urbino.

CAMACHO: As I am new to these parts, Your Excellency,
and my eyesight is not as good as it should be,
I am sorry not to have recognised you straight away,
and responded with the respect you deserve.
If only my pages had not gone and lost my best eye-glass!

PARIS: I respect the goodness of your intentions.
But tell me, are these clothes you're wearing used in Spain?

CAMACHO: When it comes to clothes,
there is nothing in Spain that's permanent;

what seems good enough one moment,
seems quite awful the next.
There was a fashionable gentleman
who kept in his attic all the old hats he
had amassed over the past forty years.
Taking them out one day,
in front of a group of prudent dressers,
he astounded everyone by revealing that
each and every hat was different.

PARIS: Here's Spanish fantasy for you!

CAMACHO: Their beauty was in being so varied,
just like Nature, which makes not a single face the same.

PARIS: So give me some idea of what the Spanish Court is like.

CAMACHO: What can I say? There are a lot of men, and a
lot of women.
Hello there!

MARINO: Yes sir…

CAMACHO: You're a pair of barbarians.

PARIS: This is a fine way of talking!

ESTACIO: This Spaniard is most odd, I would agree.

CAMACHO: Why have my gloves been perfumed with
such a vulgar amount of musk?

MENDOZA: To temper the fragrance of the myrrh.

CAMACHO: You should never overdo the musk,
it is a smell favoured by common people;
using it is like talking business with a man of letters.
Send this back immediately to the glove-maker.

PARIS: Was there ever a Spaniard like this one?

ESTACIO: As soon as he opens his mouth, Diana is going
to fall for him.
She is very capricious too, and a lover of the unusual.

PARIS: From what we have seen of him
he would certainly seem to be the perfect partner.
So, Your Lordship, how was the Spanish Court when you
left it?
In good shape, I trust.

CAMACHO: Very good indeed, sir, but also very sad.

PARIS: How so?

CAMACHO: My departure was deeply felt.
PARIS: And with good reason.
    And what, prey, is your illustrious tide?
CAMACHO: The Marquis of Mal-Odor.
PARIS: And where does your fiefdom lie?
CAMACHO: Near Cova-Ponga.
PARIS: And why has Your Lordship come
    all the way to Italy to marry?
CAMACHO: One day, when I was about to go a bed,
    I happened to see a portrait of the beautiful Diana;
    and, as you will surely appreciate as a man,
    seeing such things on the point of sleeping,
    can influence one's dreams, not to mention one's desires.
    The state of mind, and body, in which I then woke up,
    left me in no doubt that I wanted her as my wife;
    and so, putting on my breeches, I rushed post haste to Italy,
    and here I am, in all my glory, living proof that when it
                      comes to
    life decisions it is easier dealing with a picture than a
                      person.
PARIS: And is your love aware of your intentions?
CAMACHO: Oh yes, ambassadors have been going to and fro.
ESTACIO: You are clearly favoured by the heavens!
PARIS: You shall marry Diana, I have no doubt about it.
ESTACIO: This is the moment to try and win his friendship.
PARIS: Today I would like Your Lordship to come and dine
                      with me.
CAMACHO: With the greatest of pleasure.
    Hello there! Tell Mantua that I shall be eating today with
                      Urbino,
    and do try and find out from the steward if there is any
                      news from Spain;
    I haven't had a single letter in days, I'm getting gloomy.
PARIS: Spanish gravity, it's famous.
CAMACHO: Have my horses arrived yet?
MENDOZA: Only the sorrel.
PARIS: Do not worry,
    every horse of mine is a horse of yours.

CAMACHO: Let's hope they know my whims,
and show me off in all my princely splendour.
PARIS: They are the finest horses in the land.
Come on, Your Lordship.
CAMACHO: I am coming.
Tell the Duke and all the other knights gathered here in
Ferrara,
that they should not lose any appetite on account of me.
Reassure them that I am being wonderfully looked after
by Urbino,
who seems a most courteous and well-behaved gentleman
PARIS: Please, I beg of you,
you think too highly of me.
CAMACHO: Hello there!
MARINO: Yes sir...
CAMACHO: Tell the Duke to drink to my health,
for I shall do the same for him.
(*Exit.*
Enter FINEA and FLORELA.)
FLORELA: What's got over you?
Why are you flirting with me?
FINEA: Doesn't my mistress Laura do so as well?
FLORELA: Who?
FINEA: Laura.
FLORELA: With me?
FINEA: Much more blatantly besides.
And if she's like that with you,
there's no need to be so shocked
when I start courting too.
FLORELA: (She must have seen us when we were on our own
behaving like mad and foolish lovers.)
But who do you think I am?
Do you not know that I am a woman?
FINEA: Because you are a woman,
does that not mean I cannot love you?
FLORELA: Not in your sort of way.
FINEA: I do not understand
FLORELA: Your love for me seems more than just platonic.

FINEA: And what is wrong in that?
  Are you saying that someone of your learning
  is unaware of the many different forms
  of love permitted by the ancients?
  Do you not remember that Pasiphae loved a bull,
  Ciparisus a deer, and Semiramis a horse?
  Or that others have loved fishes, trees, and statues too?
  If we think of all the things and creatures
  that have inspired the love of humans,
  how could we object if a woman loves a woman?
FLORELA: But why is this more acceptable than the love
                          of men for other men?
FINEA: Because it is a pure and legitimate love.
FLORELA: I, Finea, would punish a woman for loving
                          another woman,
  especially when she starts touching me on the hand and face.
  Could you please desist immediately, Finea,
  and go and find yourself a man.
FINEA: But you are all that my soul desires.
FLORELA: And I am asking you to leave me in peace.
FINEA: You must return my love.
FLORELA: I am afraid I love Laura,
  and she can offer a different and more noble love than yours.
FINEA: That is very true.
FLORELA: In that case you have no reason to complain.
FINEA: If I were to think of you as a man,
  would you stop me from doing so?
FLORELA: (She must have overheard something; what can
                          I tell her?)
FINEA: (I am going to have to sneak tonight into her bedroom
  and try and glimpse her without her clothes on.)
  Do not look so worried, Diana,
  let us just hold hands, and go back to being friends.
  I am not another scheming Jupiter in disguise.
  (*Enter LAURA, shouting to her maid SILVANA.*)
LAURA: No, no, no, and a thousand times no.
  Just give him back his note, Silvana.
FLORELA: What note?

LAURA: Oh, it's nothing.

FLORELA: Tell me, what note?

LAURA: I did not touch it.

FLORELA: It was from Alexander, wasn't it?

LAURA: It was, but I never accepted it.

FLORELA: I am dead already!

LAURA: What is wrong?

FLORELA: I am fainting.

LAURA: Hold on to my hand.

FLORELA: Ay!

LAURA: My darling!

FINEA: As soon as you mentioned who the note was from,
 she reacted as if she had been struck by lightning;
 all the colour went from her face.

LAURA: Let's talk later.

FINEA: She did not respond like that with me,
 she went furious, that's all.

LAURA: So you found out nothing?

FINEA: But was there anything to find?
 I was reminded of a story about a gentleman so poor
 that his house had neither clothes nor furnishings.
 On discovering one day six thieves inside, he told them,
 'You must be mad. Why bother to search
 at night for what even I cannot find by day.'
 Well, I think your behaviour with Diana is equally insane.
 How can you love her, and never leave her side,
 and yet still not know whether she be man or woman?
 Do not waste more time on what is probably a delusion,
 but find out now or never one way or the other.
 While she continues to lie unconscious on the ground,
 seize the opportunity, open up her blouse,
 and stare at her breasts, if, of course, she has any.

LAURA: You are quite right; I'll start taking off her clothes.

FLORELA: Oh my God!

FINEA: Careful, she's coming round.

LAURA: My darling!

FLORELA: What on earth came over me?
 Did I reveal anything that I should not have done?

LAURA: Finea, I think it would be a good idea if
   you went to see what my father is doing.

FINEA: I shall go immediately.

LAURA: My darling Felix, we are on our own.

FLORELA: I know, Laura, and I also know too well
   what you were trying to do to me.
   May God forgive you for trying
   to uncover the secrets of my chest.
   What is it that you want of me?
   Or of Alexander? Please tell me what you want!
   If I offended you as a man,
   let us go back again to being women.
   I lied to you, Laura; I have lied;
   I am a woman. Can you not see
   how from my hair down to my feet
   I am as female as the clothes I wear?
   If I said I was a man, it was to deceive you.

LAURA: My darling Felix, there is no more need
   to invent new pretences. I no longer care.
   Whatever sex or creature you might be,
   you are my God and the light of my existence.
   (*Enter the DUKE of Ferrara and the INFANTE of Aragón.*)

DUKE: Everyone is talking about this Spaniard.

INFANTE: I hope we meet him today.

DUKE: They say his humour is extraordinary.

INFANTE: He is a guest of Alexander.

DUKE: Is that Laura?

INFANTE: Let me kiss your feet.

LAURA: Have I your permission, father, to speak to him?

DUKE: The Infante would desire this, I am sure.

LAURA: Then his wishes are mine as well.

FLORELA: Pay no attention to my sighs, Laura,
   they are just the groans of my jealous heart.

LAURA: Keep quiet, Felix, do you not realise that this
   is just a tactful ploy to keep my father happy?

FLORELA: And what if the Infante had been Alexander?

LAURA: Then I would have had to flee.

DUKE: Since Laura has decided to be seen in public, I
   would like you, Infante, to take your seat besides her.

(*They all sit down.*)

INFANTE: (My eyes would perhaps be better employed
 turned towards Diana, whose celebrated mind
 both intrigues me and holds the key to Laura's fate.)
 (*Enter a MAID.*)

MAID: A Spaniard has come to see you.

DUKE: And who is this man?

MAID: The Marquis of Mal-Odor.

DUKE: Doubtless this is the same person
 whose sense of humour has been so greatly praised.
 Please, Laura, do not leave the room,
 there is no need to be shy in front of strangers.
 He has only come, they say, to court your friend Diana.
 (*Enter CAMACHO and PAGES.*)

CAMACHO: Forgive me, Your Excellency, for being so late.
 I have been held up by another Duke, and thus
 have failed to honour the noble obligation of coming
 here immediately to kiss your great and illustrious feet.

LAURA: He has been well brought up!

INFANTE: What a gracious presence!

DUKE: Your Lordship is a thousand times welcome.
 Hello there, some more seats please!

CAMACHO: I am happy to sit anywhere.

FLORELA: Who ever would have thought
 I would have attracted such a man as him!

CAMACHO: Let me kiss your hand, fair Duchess.

LAURA: I am happy to oblige.

FLORELA: The thought that it is me he loves
 disturbs me somewhat.

CAMACHO: You are, I presume, the famous Diana,
 the one who everyone calls variously 'the Divine',
 'the Muse', 'the Sage', 'the Sphinx in human form'?

FLORELA: I am Diana, and I am answerable only
 to the Grand Duke and my Lady Laura.

CAMACHO: Now I can see that your fame
 does you scant justice.
 You are even gentler and more beautiful
 than anyone had led me to believe.

In Spain there were two things above all
that were said of you.

FLORELA: Only two?

CAMACHO: One was your divine and subtle mind,
the other your perfect and incomparable beauty.
I have crossed the seas only for the chance of seeing you,
for there must be something in my blood
that makes me always drawn to prodigies of nature.
Why, I would even go to Troy, if Helen were still there.

INFANTE: How delightful to love someone for their fame
alone!
I hope Your Excellency will make his stay here worthwhile.

DUKE: I shall do my very best to help him.

CAMACHO: Hello there! Is there a page around?

MARINO: Yes, sir.

CAMACHO: Could you go and fetch the
present I brought his Excellency from Spain.

INFANTE: Is it some rare object?

CAMACHO: No, no, a mere bagatelle;
it's just some little fountain in jasper and marble.
But here it comes, in different sections I am afraid;
you shall not see it at its best until...

DUKE: You are obviously a man of exquisite taste;
we shall find an excellent home for it.

CAMACHO: It is a consummate object, I agree.

DUKE: What does it represent?

CAMACHO: The Roman woman who is famed the world over
for being virtuous and foolish at the same time.

FLORELA: How can a person be both virtuous and foolish?

CAMACHO: Surely you of all people must
know that I am talking about Lucretia,
the ancient heroine who killed herself
after saying she had been raped –
a virtuous deed, but a foolish loss of life.

FLORELA: Since her death was avenged by so much
tainted blood,
her personal loss was small compared to what Rome gained.

CAMACHO: Now is not the time for arguing with you,
for I see, from all the posters,

that you shall soon be doing so with
all the great brains currently at this court.
I would not want to tire you out beforehand,
so allow me just to say that this fountain
portrays Lucretia falling on her sword,
which in my opinion was a tragic waste of beauty.

DUKE: It would be a great pleasure if the Marquis dined
with me;
and I willingly allow you two ladies to entertain him
afterwards.

LAURA: That is very generous of you!

CAMACHO: I am deeply indebted to you.

DUKE: There is no need for you to go, Infante;
come and dine with us as well.

INFANTE: I am most honoured.

DUKE: Come and sit next to me, Marquis;
I am relying on you to cheer me up a little.
(*Exit all, except LAURA and FLORELA.*)

LAURA: Have you got over your anger yet?

FLORELA: Your beauty makes it impossible for me to do so.
If I only I could go back to being a woman,
then everything would be fine; I would be your servant
Diana
and be forced to keep quiet and respect your every wish.
But if I persist in being a man, which is what I really am,
then how can I not kill myself knowing that there
is nothing that will stop you tonight from seeing Alexander?

LAURA: Dearest Felix, if you really want me not to see him,
I suggest you go instead, and pretend that you are me, so
that you can tell Alexander anything you want to.

FLORELA: God in all his justice must be using you as his
spokesman,
as if he wanted himself to temper my rival's passions.
You must think of me Laura as some jealous fool,
but I have never known of jealousy without foolishness
as well,
and besides the qualities I love and value in you are
those that make me envious and jealous all the time.

Perhaps it would be better if we went together to Alexander,
because I am frightened of what I might say if on my own.
But listen, the Duke is calling you, you must go and join
him.

LAURA: So you find that being a man is a burden to you?

FLORELA: No, good God no! Because otherwise I could
not have you as my wife.

LAURA: (*Aside.*) He really is a man then! If only I knew
what to do to find the final proof.

FLORELA: (*Aside.*) I sigh because I am not a man,
I almost wish now that I was.

(*Enter ALEXANDER by night, with shield and sword.*)

ALEXANDER: I have come here because I want to know
whether love is a lawful and munificent ruler
or just a tyrant misleading our souls and our bodies.
With every obstacle placed in the path of my desires,
my ever darker mind is turning into a maze of queries,
and I can only wonder if anyone will win Laura's heart,
or if all this is just a vengeful scheme thought up by Florela,
who seems to have put a curse on my every endeavour.
I try to find a way head, but see no other path than those
that end in defeat, humiliation and Laura's mocking smile.
As the labyrinth expands, my hope is fading to the
faintest flicker,
and soon I shall enter a darkness from which there is no
escape.
But, my God, there is movement on the balcony, I hear
her voice.
Be brave, Alexander, approach her with your trembling
steps!

Florela and Laura appear on the balcony.

FLORELA: That seems like Alexander to me.

LAURA: Well go and speak to him,
I give you my permission.

FLORELA: I kiss your feet;
but why are you going away?

LAURA: I shall wait for you in the corridor;
I leave my good name in your hands.
(*Exit.*)

FLORELA: I cannot believe she has left me on my own.
Hello, is that a gallant knight down there
wandering in the shadows?
Are you Alexander, the famous Duke of Mantua?

ALEXANDER: I am Alexander, and though I cannot offer you
the world that my namesake conquered
I can offer the precious gift that is my soul.

FLORELA: I thank you for your kind words,
but cannot as yet thank you for your deeds,
for so far you have done little to prove yourself.

ALEXANDER: I have failed to do so, my lady,
because for some reason you have
decided to test out my love for you
not with proofs of manliness
but with a maze of intellectual games
that have tied my simple mind in knots.
If only you had thought of me as another Jason
and I would have brought you back the Golden Fleece,
and conquered bulls who lashed at me with tongues of fire!
If only...

FLORELA: Do not bother to continue,
just answer this one question.
Are not you the same flatterer
who, in Mantua, had loved Florela?

ALEXANDER: Me? Florela?

FLORELA: Look how he denies it!
And have you forgotten as well
that after having had your way
you deceived her with the promise of marriage?

ALEXANDER: I promised Florela?
The person who told you this is lying,
and wanted obviously to make you hate me.

FLORELA: (*Aside.*) Great god in heaven, what shall I do?
I have had what I deserved in coming here,
and do not know which guise to turn to now.
Shall I just tell him outright who I am?
But if I do so, I shall shatter this whole edifice
of deceit on which I have built my hopes.

For I suspect that if Laura really knows I am a woman,
her disillusionment will lead her straight to Alexander's
arms.

ALEXANDER: There are people coming; I shall be back
later.

(*Enter CAMACHO with a lantern and shield.*)

CAMACHO: My servants have all abandoned me,
they soon tired of all their 'no sirs' and 'yes sirs'.
A nobleman's life is not what it used to be,
there's no more respect or dignity.
The Duke gulped his dinner down in a flash,
then fell into a deep and snoring slumber.
The Infante made his excuses, then fucked off too,
leaving me completely to my own devices.
If it weren't for the moon, and this handy
little lantern that I happened to find,
I would be stumbling around on hands and knees like
someone hurled from Fortune's wheel.
Well, I think I must have reached now
what my master called the 'flirting terrace'.

ALEXANDER: Who's that bloody fool with the light?
Put it out, or cover it up and get the hell out of here!

CAMACHO: I am staying exactly as I am.
You might be some noble lord, for all I know,
but there's never any excuse for showing no respect.

ALEXANDER: If you don't tell me who you are,
I promise by God that I'll grab your hat and lamp
and hurl them right across the garden.

CAMACHO: I am the Marquis Don Lucas
and if you take away my lamp,
I shall swirl my cape, prick up my moustache,
and become so red and swollen with anger
that you too shall be visiting the garden –
to try and collect all the pieces from your nose.

ALEXANDER: You're not Camacho are you?

CAMACHO: You're not Alexander?

ALEXANDER: You're a lunatic and a liability.
What the hell do you think you're doing here?

CAMACHO: This is turning into a real hoot!
    Everything's in such a tangle,
    that we've started tripping over each other.
    You make me laugh, you really do!
ALEXANDER: Keep your voice down,
    I have come here to speak to Laura.
    She's on the balcony.
CAMACHO: Laura?
ALEXANDER: And Diana too, I suspect.
CAMACHO: Diana, Diana, it's me your noble suitor!
    I am waiting here below the gates of paradise,
    in the full light of the moon, as we had agreed.
FLORELA: Who is that?
CAMACHO: The Marquis Don Lucas.
FLORELA: You are far too early,
    and I cannot speak to you now.
    But your chivalrous attention deserves some reward.
CAMACHO: I long ardently for some token from your fair
                                                    hands.
FLORELA: I have written something on a piece of paper;
    but tell me first if you are as discreet
    as Laura says you are.
CAMACHO: She has told you the truth.
FLORELA: Well, here it is. Goodbye.
CAMACHO: Can't you stay for a moment?
FLORELA: I cannot.
ALEXANDER: Has she gone?
CAMACHO: Diana has gone, yes.
ALEXANDER: And Laura?
CAMACHO: She was already indoors.
ALEXANDER: What did she give you?
CAMACHO: Another bloody piece of paper.
ALEXANDER: Well, you were lucky.
CAMACHO: I deserved more.
ALEXANDER: Well, read it then, as you have so
    thoughtfully brought a light.
CAMACHO: What? Right here?
ALEXANDER: Why ever not, for God's sake?

CAMACHO: I shall begin.
  (*He reads the piece of paper.*)
  'I love the one who loves me not,
  I do not love the one who loves me.'
ALEXANDER: Well, go on then.
CAMACHO: That's it. There's nothing more.
ALEXANDER: Nothing more?
CAMACHO: What more do you expect?
  The concept of 'more' is little known around here,
  what we get instead is quite a lot of 'less'.
  Any rate, I've got all that I need from that piece of paper.
ALEXANDER: Were you able to understand it?
CAMACHO: Every bloody word, it was a synch.
  You soon get used to riddles
  when you're in a place riddled with them.
  The message is completely clear:
  she loves me, but thinks I do not love her;
  and for my sake she has rejected many other would-be
                                                    lovers.
ALEXANDER: You poor deluded fool!
CAMACHO: What on earth's foolish about
  seeing everything on the bright side?
  Well I bet you won't be calling me a fool
  when I tell you now what I have gone and done:
  I have found a most ingenious way of
  sneaking into the labyrinth not only
  a month's supply at least of food,
  but also tinder, flint and stone
  so that we can light a fire as well.
ALEXANDER: And how have you done all this?
CAMACHO: Simple. I presented to the Duke a pretty fountain,
  which came in several pieces for easy transportation.
  Well, he has behaved exactly as I had hoped,
  and has decided to place the object in the small patio
  that has been built at the very entrance to the labyrinth.
  Assembling the fountain will enable me to hide within it
  some rare and excellent wines, the finest Parma hams,
  a delectable range of cheeses, pastries, conserves, and so on.

ALEXANDER: You are a genius!

CAMACHO: I think that even if we lose ourselves inside,
we shall have enough of everything to live in style
for at least a month or two.

ALEXANDER: I want to embrace you.

CAMACHO: Well do it quickly, I hear soldiers coming.

ALEXANDER: Let's run.

CAMACHO: Laura shall soon be yours,
and I shall have the mastery of labyrinths and puzzles!

End of Act Two.

ACT THREE

Enter PARIS of Urbino and ESTACIO.

PARIS: Tell me, Estacio, the worst.
    What is the labyrinth's final form?
ESTACIO: From what I have been told,
    by various nameless sources,
    its interior is almost a copy of
    the one built by Daedalus in Crete.
    The only difference is the roof,
    which has succeeded in locking
    out every little trace of light.
PARIS: I am sure we shall find
    some scientific brain capable
    of sneaking light into the darkest places.
    But describe in greater detail
    the structure of this labyrinth.
ESTACIO: Putting together all the different
    accounts that I have heard,
    I have deduced…
PARIS: Well, please get on with it.
ESTACIO: …that in the midst of gardens
    which bravely evoke not only
    the Hesperides but the Elysian Fields,
    as if the architect's intention was
    to suggest the celestial heights
    to which Daedalus soared with Icarus
    on fleeing afterwards from Crete…
PARIS: Oh, for God's sake…
ESTACIO: Well, these gardens provide the setting
    for a labyrinth of circular construction
    that is five hundred metres in diameter,
    and is ringed within by so many paths
    that the whole is like a giant astrolabe
    that has all gone wrong, so that all the arcs
    not only fail to complete a circle
    but also double back upon themselves,

creating endless loops that all lead nowhere.
Each path, moreover, has so many
doors and openings leading off it,
and so many walls that block its way,
that one of the builders with whom I spoke
reckoned that after only fifty metres
a person could easily get lost, and spend
at least a month without finding any exit.
Such, he said, is the nature of this Gordian Knot
that even when you think an end is in sight
you are merely metres from where you started.
And even with the help of a torch, he claimed,
or of skylights such as those that Daedalus built,
a man could still lose his way, as indeed did happen
to the architect himself, who decided to put
his ingenious construction to the test,
and ended up wandering until dawn,
when finally his exhausted cries were heard,
as he lay shocked and in despair upon the ground.
A thousand lives could well be wasted before
anyone succeeds in penetrating to the centre,
where the lucky man will find a palace which
belies its wooden structure by glowing with a coat
of gold that extends from floor to ceiling.
Here Laura, with her father, will wait seven
days to reward the victor with her fiery beauty.
But, if you ask for my opinion, not even
such a prospect would make me risk life and sanity
while undertaking so impossible a quest.

PARIS: What you have said has made me gloomier than ever;
but, hush now, Laura's father and his court are already here.
The time has come for the second stage of our strange
ordeal –
the moment when we pit our wits against Diana.

ESTACIO: Strange is certainly the word to
describe a debate headed by a woman.

PARIS: I am terrified to take part in it.
It's difficult enough trying to win Laura's hand
without having to compete as well for Apollo's crown.

ESTACIO: Look at Diana over there, she has already placed
the laurels on her head.

PARIS: How well the green sets off her rosy cheeks!
(*The DUKE, ALEXANDER, the INFANTE, two MACE-
BEARERS, LAURA, FINEA and FLORELA enter the room,
to the accompaniment of hornpipes. FLORELA, crowned by
laurels, takes her seat behind a table. CAMACHO enters
soon afterwards.*)

FLORELA: Most illustrious Duke and noble princes,
I hope you shall forgive me for not having any of
the preliminary speeches that should by right
accompany such a solemn ceremony as this.
My gifts for praising would seem but small
when compared with the sea of minds
that stretches before me in this great hall.
So, without further ado, and begging once
more your pardon, I declare the debate now open.

ALEXANDER: My God, I do not believe what I am seeing.

CAMACHO: Why are you staring like that?

ALEXANDER: That is not Diana.

CAMACHO: If it isn't her, who else can it be?

ALEXANDER: It's Florela, you Spanish dupe!
The one they call the Mantuan Sibyl:
love is certainly persistent;
it maintains its vigil even when others sleep.

CAMACHO: You better be quiet, she's looking your way.

ALEXANDER: Everything has suddenly become clear.
This whole complex game that we are playing
is but a ruse of Florela's to hinder Laura's marriage.

CAMACHO: She's started speaking again.

ALEXANDER: Has ever deceit been as elaborate as this?

FLORELA: My lady Laura, fearful of insulting in any way
the men who bring such glory to this land of Italy,
has, as you well know, submitted you all to a
competition in three parts designed to test your intellect
and ingenuity rather than your fighting skills.
A riddle has been set, and answers have been given;
but Laura's hand is still far from being won.

I have been appointed now to a task to which
I am but poorly suited – the task of taking you all on
in the debate that immediately precedes the labyrinth...
But this is what I have been asked to do, and I have no other
choice but to tell you now the subject of our debate:
The motion I propose is that women are no less capable
than men in matters of government, war, and the sciences.

ALEXANDER: With the permission of Your Excellency the
Duke,
and of all you honourable gentlemen, and beautiful
and wise ladies that are gathered here today,
I would argue with Diana – and God knows
only too well how it pains me to have to say this –
that women, sadly, are but imperfect creatures
whom Nature had never at first envisaged.
And when, finally, God decided to create Eve,
it was simply as a means to perpetuate the species.
Thus, as women's role is purely reproductive,
and they are little more than matter,
how is it possible that they can perform
the lofty duties associated with the first
and highest form of Nature that is man.

FLORELA: All I need say to refute this line of argument
is to point out that if Nature really did think
so poorly of women, then it has no right to do so,
for without women humanity would not exist,
and we would not be having any form of argument at all.

ALEXANDER: I continue to maintain that women are an
afterthought of Nature.

DUKE: Diana's cleverness is remarkable.

ALEXANDER: Nature, according to Aristotle,
always wants to create what is perfect. I refer you to his
comments on heaven and earth,
youth and old age, and the reproduction of animals, all
of which are from Book Two of *De Anima,*
chapters five, two and fourteen respectively.
It thus goes without saying that
if women are the most imperfect of humans
then Nature had not originally wanted to create them.

FLORELA: Since your argument rests on the assumption
　　that women are less perfect than men,
　　I would not call yours an argument
　　but rather a blind prejudice.
ALEXANDER: I shall prove my point!
FLORELA: And I shall deny it!
ALEXANDER: First, the inferiority of women in relation
　　　　　　　　　　　　　　　　　to men
　　is shown by the scarcity of famous women
　　known to us from history.
　　Secondly, Aristotle himself, in his discussion of
　　the reproduction of animals, states quite clearly
　　that if a woman succeeds in having the qualities of a man,
　　this is by accident rather than by design.
　　I refer you also to Aristotle's *The Politics,* Book Seven,
　　　　　　　　　　　　　　　　Chapter Four.
FLORELA: St Thomas Aquinas convincingly refutes this
　　　　　　　　　　　　　　　　point
　　in the commentary on Aristotle featured in his *Summa
　　　　　　　　　　　　　　　　Theologae.*
　　I refer in particular to the first part of Section Ninety-two.
　　In any case the philosophers and theologians who describe
　　woman as imperfect, and believe that female intelligence
　　　　　　　　　　　　　　　　is accidental
　　have all been men who have merely wanted to keep
　　　　　　　　　　　　　　　women in their place.
　　I would argue that women, far from being imperfect,
　　are not only responsible for perpetuating Nature in all its
　　　　　　　　　　　　　　　　glory,
　　but also for providing the element of spiritual beauty
　　　　　　　　　　　　　　　necessary
　　to give wholeness and perfection to the world we live in.
　　Remember when God gave Adam a companion in the
　　　　　　　　　　　　　　　form of Eve,
　　He told him that 'it is not good for a man to be all on
　　　　　　　　　　　　　　　his own',
　　and that 'the human race can never be perfect without a
　　　　　　　　　　　　　　　woman'.

ALEXANDER: Three important points need to be made
on the subject of the equality of souls.
The soul is the first part of the body to be born;
and Adam was the first human being.
Therefore it follows that the first and greatest
soul is man's, and that having such a soul
makes men more suited to intellectual activities
than women... But, I am sorry, I have lost
the thread of my argument. I give in.

INFANTE: In that case, with your permission,
I would like to make my own contribution
to this debate. I sustain that woman
is less perfect than man for the following reason:
if an imperfect man is unsuited to letters and sciences,
then it goes without saying that a woman is even more
unsuited.

FLORELA: If that is the level of your debate,
then I am afraid I am going to have
to speak in a simple language
appropriate to your intellectual capacities.
Your argument has no validity whatsoever
because, for want of convincing proof to the contrary,
we have already proved that the souls
of men and women are the same.

INFANTE: Give me a chance, I too have read my Aquinas,
and indeed would like to refer you now to
the second sentence of the twenty-first point
made in the second part of the first book of the *Summa*.
In this it is stated that that the soul is the
form that is allied to the matter which is the body.
Thus we can deduce that those with better bodies
have better souls, as is shown in the case of Adam,
who, as we all know, had a nobler and better
proportioned body than Eve.

FLORELA: I concede that Adam was born before Eve,
and that the soul and the body are intimately connected.
However, to go on, as you do, to infer from this
a whole system of human perfection based on
the relationship between body and soul is patently absurd.

INFANTE: I shall prove my point.

FLORELA: I look forward to hearing your proof.

INFANTE: The very moment someone is born
    the soul determines the type
    of body appropriate to his stature.
    Thus, to take the example of my fellow competitor
                                        Alexander,
    the soul endowed him with a fine and imposing physique
    knowing that he was going to grow up as a duke.

FLORELA: I agree that the soul communicates with
    the body from the instance of birth.
    However, the body, as St Thomas Aquinas himself said,
    is always subject to the accidents of Nature,
    which is why talking about the body is a very different
    matter to talking about the human soul.
    When it comes to the soul, Aquinas plainly states that
    all individuals display an equal perfection.
    If we were speaking about the body, however,
    I would argue that accidental circumstances have
    determined that women are more perfect than men
    for being on the whole far more beautiful.

CAMACHO: Good God almighty,
    she certainly knows her stuff from
    A to P, and from P to Z!
    It's curtains for Plato!

PARIS: Look, with the permission of you all,
    I would like to give this argument
    a firmer basis in fact and science.
    First of all, I want Diana to tell me
    what is the first part of the body to be formed.

FLORELA: How do you want me to answer this?
    Do you want me to give you a full account of
    Hippocrates's views on the matter?
    Or do you want me to stick with Aristotoles,
    whom all of you seem to have read,
    at least in part? I suspect, however, that
    Hippocrates might be too technical for you,
    so I shall just repeat the Aristotelian view
    that the heart is the primary organ,

for it is with the blood flowing from its arteries
that the body is given the heat which is life itself.
PARIS: The point I wanted to make is that if the body
can be divided up into organs of primary and lesser
importance,
so too can the soul, which surely has parts
that make a person more disposed to certain activities
than others.
It is my contention that woman lacks
the special temperament needed for the sciences.
FLORELA: Oh how easily you men throw yourself into
deep waters!
Well, Paris, there is a question I want to ask you.
Do you know what humour is best suited to the intellect?
PARIS: I do.
FLORELA: What is it then?
PARIS: The melancholic humour.
FLORELA: I disagree with you.
PARIS: But the proof is in Aristotle. According to him
all the greatest poets, philosophers and artists,
from Lisander of Greece to Socrates, Plato, and Empedocles,
were all of a melancholic disposition.
And why are old people thought to be so wise?
Because sadness is their dominant humour.
CAMACHO: Now I know why I'm always so sad.
However, if the saddest people are the wisest,
does this mean that those who haven't got a penny
are the greatest geniuses of them all?
FLORELA: Paris, I agree that melancholy is often
an accompaniment to genius,
but wisdom itself comes rather from experience.
Furthermore, if we were to find an
explanation of intellect in the humours,
then we would have to quote Galenus,
who believed that melancholy, in those
of intellectual disposition, alternated with
bile and pure blood – the latter being
the dominant characteristics of millions of women.

Finally, since you all appear so keen to
bring in Aristotle, I would remind you
that this greatest of ancient philosophers
said himself that those of soft skin
and tender complexion were the people
most likely to have a superior intellect.
With this statement I think we can safely conclude
that women have the greatest aptitude
for sciences and letters.

CAMACHO: That was brilliantly put; and I don't want
anyone else now to argue with this
or continue to dispute truths that
are obvious and conclusively proved.
And if anyone is silly enough to do so
then I suggest that they look more
carefully at all those boring old books
they are so fond of quoting.
Look in Textor, in Estobeus, or in Seneca,
or in any of the great ancient and modern authors
and you will find that every period of history
has produced innumerable women who
have achieved fame in war, peace, and government.
Take the example of Deborah, the prophetess
who ruled over the Jews; or of Tomiris,
who held command in Scythia and Persia;
think of Cenobia in Syria, Valasca in Bohemia,
Candaces in Ethiopia, Helerna in ancient Italy.
And need I mention Amalasunta, ruler of the Goths,
or Cleopatra, the celebrated Queen of Egypt?
And as for sciences and letters, who could possibly
have been as knowledgeable as Aspasia, Manto, Casandra,
and Targelia, let alone the Muses, all of whom
of course were women? Let us not forget as well
that Catalan woman – Juliana I think she's called –
who has recently retired to a Spanish convent,
and is said to have taught publicly in Paris
from the age of fourteen, and to have published
books that have left scholars speechless.

And what man could have done what that woman
did a few years back in Florence and rescued a Duke's
son from the teeth of a lion? Think too of that
beautiful Countess of Castile who managed
so ingeniously to get the great Feman Gómez out of prison?
Or what about that Galician heroine who caused
so much havoc in La Coruna with her shield and sword?
When it comes to praising women,
I could go on endlessly; but there's just one more
thing I want to say in their defence.
Namely that if any one of you here persists in
calling them imperfect, I'll resolve the conflict
with traditional male means, and bring a
bit of theatrical excitement to this tedious discussion
by resorting to a full-scale duel with lances and horses.
I've had enough now; if anyone wants a fight,
you can come and find me in my country retreat.
If I'm in a good mood I'll be lying pissed
under the shadow of a tree; if I'm not
I shall be at home, eating lunch, if it's midday,
or snoring soundly in my bed, if night time's come.
I must be going now, my bile is rising!
(*Exit CAMACHO.*)

DUKE: Try and stop him, do not let him leave.

LAURA: It is too late now, I doubt that he will be coming
back.

DUKE: Gentlemen, the debate is over.
As you know well,
what happens next is that Laura and I,
with two of our retinue,
will be waiting for you inside the labyrinth.
Go now and prove yourself in this final test.
(*Exit everyone except ALEXANDER.*)

ALEXANDER: Is there anyone who would want to be in
my position?
Is there anyone more unfortunate than I am now?
Florela, whom I thought I had left behind in Mantua,
is now here in Ferrara transformed into an avenging beast,

while Laura seems to hate me, and wish me gone forever.
With the labyrinth that has been built to crush my hopes,
Florela has carried vengeance to its cruel conclusion.
In my predicament I see myself as the parched and hungry
Tantalus, up to his neck in water that he can never drink,
almost touching with his mouth fruit that he can never eat.
I have reached a state from which there is no escape,
for if the soul itself is no different to a labyrinth,
how can I ever free myself from my darkest worries?
(*Enter CAMACHO.*)

CAMACHO: Having recovered somewhat from my outburst,
I said to myself I shall go and look for Alexander,
and now I find him looking as lost and pathetic
as a tiny boat tossed up and down in the high seas.
Are you going to continue your pacing, or
are you going to do as you're supposed to
and follow in the Duke's footsteps?

ALEXANDER: I am in a mind to go straight back to Ferrara,
and were I not held so tightly in love's grip,
would do so right away:
this harpy who calls herself Diana
has certainly done her best to
prevent Laura from ever being mine.

CAMACHO: All the more reason therefore
to try and thwart her plans
and pursue Laura with
greater determination than ever.

ALEXANDER: My love for her will be the end of me;
but for her sake I am prepared to
die a thousand times…

CAMACHO: I've heard that before.
But hurry up, the guards are calling for you at
the labyrinth's gates.

ALEXANDER: I imagine the Duke is just about to enter.

CAMACHO: Yes, he and his small group will soon be
going in with their torches to take up their positions.

ALEXANDER: Today I am determined to succeed at all costs.

CAMACHO: You're going to, don't worry.
Remember I've placed the fake fountain

in the labyrinth's vestibule, where there's
still enough light to see properly.
You'll find a little keyhole in the sculpted panel,
cleverly disguised within Lucretia's navel.
Turn this little key which I shall give you now,
and everything shall be revealed –
torches, flints, bread, wine, cheese, ham,
and three hundred other things besides.
Take out everything you need,
and you can then go happily on your way.

ALEXANDER: What a stroke of luck that the
Duke had your fountain placed in
so convenient a position.
Nonetheless I would be happier still
if you came in shortly after me,
so that I can go and look for you,
and have some company.

CAMACHO: Me sir? You're joking, I hope.
Have I ever shown any interest in Laura?

ALEXANDER: So my own wishes are less important to you
than your lack of feelings for Laura?

CAMACHO: Of course not. I'm just concerned
about what would happen if I got
to Laura before you did.

ALEXANDER: Don't worry,
I shall make sure you do not.
We shall stay together until
we reach the stage where
we think we are almost there.
Then we shall split up:
I shall continue to the inner chamber
and you shall go your own way.

CAMACHO: I'm a Spaniard, I've no other choice
but to accept so terrible a deal as this.
Let's get going then.

ALEXANDER: I shall go first.

CAMACHO: If I get left behind in the labyrinth,
I'd be grateful if you sent a letter to Toledo,

letting everyone know that
I'm so highly thought of in Ferrara
that I've been mummified.
(*Exit.*
Enter LAURA, FLORELA, and the DUKE of Ferrara,
followed by FINEA and LIRANO, a servant.)
FLORELA: With Your Excellency's permission,
   I would rather we did not leave the vestibule just yet.
DUKE: Is there something that worries you?
FLORELA: Yes, sire there is.
   I am not very happy about this fountain.
   I think there might be something inside it.
DUKE: Knowing how sharp and perceptive you are,
   I am prepared to have my servant Lirano break it open.
FLORELA: You put too much faith in me, sire;
   but I feel that it should be checked.
DUKE: As I remember, it comes in sections.
   We shall have it taken apart,
   and see whether it is made of jasper or of treachery.
FLORELA: Had someone done the same at Troy,
   and looked inside the wooden horse,
   where the Grecian forces hid,
   an entire city would have been saved.
DUKE: Do you think the fountain is another foreigner's trick?
   It was given to us, after all, by that curious
   Spaniard, the Marquis of Mal-Odor.
FLORELA: Spaniards are famous for their clever ingenuity.
   I was suspicious of him from the start.
LIRANO: The fountain is so light that I can almost lift it.
LAURA: When I saw only two people carrying it,
   I thought it could not be either of jasper or of marble.
DUKE: There seems to be a hairline crack
   running right through the middle of the relief.
LAURA: Isn't that a keyhole?
FLORELA: Try and prise the whole thing open.
LIRANO: A hammer and chisel should do the job nicely.
   There, I've opened it.
FLORELA: Is it jasper?

FINEA: I hardly think so, my lady.

FLORELA: So my suspicions were justified, were they not?

LIRANO: Look what we have here. Flints and torches.

FINEA: There's wax as well.

DUKE: Who ever would have thought it?

LIRANO: My God, a flagon of wine.

FINEA: And here's a whole ham.

LIRANO: And here are some jars.

FINEA: They are full of food.

FLORELA: Wax and torches, and
    enough to eat for many days.
    This is a serious matter.

LAURA: You have to admire the ingenuity.

DUKE: It is a wretched trick if you ask me!

LAURA: But thank goodness we have Diana
    to outwit its perpetrator!

DUKE: I want everything inside the fountain
    to be cleared away immediately.
    (*Exit the DUKE, followed by LIRANO and FINEA.*)

FLORELA: Look at the fountain now.
    I cannot believe that this beautiful object
    in shining marble and green jasper
    turns out to be just a hoax in white plaster.
    Oh, Laura, I am quite convinced now
    that our days together are nearly over!

LAURA: Why do you say that, my darling?

FLORELA: Because love will always find a way
    through the darkest labyrinth;
    there is nothing more ingenious than love.

LAURA: But even if there was somebody
    who had all the luck, skills,
    and ingenuity to achieve this,
    I swear to you, with all my heart,
    that there is no-one who will
    ever take away what there is between us.
    Either I shall be yours for ever,
    or else I shall die distraught.

FLORELA: I want you to know, Laura,
  that I too shall die should you ever leave me.
  I want you to know that I am now entirely yours,
  and that you hold my life in the pupils of your eyes.
  Oh, Laura, if I had countless souls,
  I would want them joined together,
  and threaded through your eyelashes,
  so as to guard your eyes for ever.
  I want you to know that everything up to now
  has merely been a means to keep you mine:
  should any of your suitors succeed in reaching you,
  then please, I beg of you, turn him straight away.
LAURA: My darling, you have to trust me,
  you know how much I love you.
FLORELA: But you must know as well, my beloved Laura,
  that another person's love can never be trusted
  unless it is equal to or greater than one's own.
LAURA: But yours is the love that is unequal,
  for no-one could love somebody as much as I do you.
FLORELA: Then how do you consider yourself now?
LAURA: As your wife.
FLORELA: In that case I trust you.
LAURA: Go now and have a look for any other hidden
                                                surprises.
FLORELA: I shall, and in the process die for want of
                                          looking at you.
  (*Exit FLORELA.*
  Enter FINEA.)
FINEA: This is truly amazing this love affair of yours!
  Can you not even restrain yourself in the middle of a
                                                labyrinth?
  Well let me warn you that your time is limited.
  Strange and ingenious plots seem to have been hatched,
  and it surely cannot be long before you have to marry.
  You must try and stop loving this Phoenix or Felix,
  or whatever he or she calls himself.
LAURA: But how can you just forget someone who appears
  wiser and more beautiful than Apollo must have done
  when striding through the Elysian Fields?

But let us change the subject. You still have not told me
what happened last night between you and my beloved.
FINEA: I have still to get over the embarrassment.
　　I can hardly believe that I could have been so daring
　　or foolhardy to get right up to his bed and lift the silk
　　　　　　　　　　　　　　　　　　　　　　　　　coverlet.
LAURA: What, what? What's this you're telling me?
FINEA: I knew you would be shocked.
　　I lifted the bed cover
　　it was an awful thing to do, I know.
LAURA: And what else?
　　 What else, for God's sake?
FINEA: As soon as I touched the cover
　　he stirred, and muttered in his sleepy state:
　　'Is that my Laura? Is that my beautiful Minotaur
　　who awaits me in the labyrinth of desire?'
　　'No, I am just a little bull girl,' I whispered while
　　managing to get a good glimpse...
LAURA: Yes, yes?
FINEA: '...of his feet.'
LAURA: Were you not more daring than that?
FINEA: Why should I have been?
　　Was it not enough just to see
　　the feet in all their naked beauty?
LAURA: My dear Finea, simply seeing the feet
　　cannot reveal what I want to know
　　But tell me more, tell me more:
　　what part of him did you touch?
FINEA: You really are behaving strangely!
　　If all you wanted was visual proof
　　why are you asking me these things?
　　The feet of a woman are very different
　　from those of a man, and there's an end to it.
LAURA: The Duke is calling.
FINEA: I better be quiet then,
　　in any case I have said too much already.
LAURA: But please make me clear on just one point.
　　Can I love this person?
FINEA: It is not impossible.

(*Exit LAURA and FINEA.*
Enter the INFANTE with a SERVANT.)

SERVANT: So you are determined to go ahead with this?

INFANTE: Today I shall enter the labyrinth,
which some are saying is the greatest test
that the mind can possibly endure.

SERVANT: And what help did your philosopher friend give
you?

INFANTE: He devised a scheme of such ingenuity
that I think of him now with a laurel crown on his head.
Have you not heard how Theseus
survived the Cretan labyrinth with the aid of a thread?
Well I am carrying one on me too.

SERVANT: In that case your friend cannot be as clever as
you think.

Have you not heard how everyone who enters the labyrinth
has to be searched from head to foot; and that the guards
would not hesitate in stripping a king if this be necessary?

INFANTE: Well they can do whatever they want to me,
and they would still be staring at the thread
without being able to see it at all.

SERVANT: To see something without seeing it
would indeed be an ingenious trick.

INFANTE: The beauty of the whole thing is
that it is so remarkably ingenious
while being so marvellously simple.
The secret lies in this splendid jacket
that I am wearing, with its braid
of the strongest and most costly silk.
Well the braid itself, which doubles
around the body several times,
and comes right up to the sleeves,
can, when loosened, be unwound
to form a single ball of thread.
Isn't that remarkable?

SERVANT: It is a stroke of genius, I agree.
Come on, the guards are calling now.
You can now enter the labyrinth
in the knowledge that you will not get lost.

INFANTE: Love clearly wants me to be the victor of this
contest.

   The guards are coming.

   (*Enter three GUARDS with harquebuses.*)

FIRST GUARD: One of the lady's suitors has arrived.

SECOND GUARD: Who goes there?

INFANTE: The Infante of Aragón.

THIRD GUARD: What brings you here, Your Highness?

INFANTE: I want to take part in this great exploit.

FIRST GUARD: You know the rules?

INFANTE: I do.

FIRST GUARD: Then I must ask you to
   go and be searched in that room over there.

INFANTE: I quite understand.

THIRD GUARD: I apologise Your Highness for the
inconvenience.

INFANTE: I am happy to do anything for love.

   (*Enter ALEXANDER and CAMACHO.*)

CAMACHO: The guards are already at the gates;
   you can proceed to the next stage.

ALEXANDER: Excuse me, guards!

FIRST GUARD: Hail Prince Alexander!
   Hail great Duke of Mantua!

ALEXANDER: For the glory of winning
   the hand of the lady Laura
   I have come now to undertake
   this most dangerous of enterprises.

CAMACHO: Guards!

FIRST GUARD: Who's that?

CAMACHO: I am...but surely you must recognise me?

FIRST GUARD: Your Lordship, please tell us who you are.

CAMACHO: I am Don Lucas of Galicia.

SECOND GUARD: The Marquis?

CAMACHO: The very same.

SECOND GUARD: And does Your Lordship also want to
   take part in this great contest?

CAMACHO: Are you saying I lack courage or brain power?
   Everything's always worth a try, that's my motto.
   Let me tell you this story about how one day,

in Spain, I went hunting for partridges with a group of
             friends.
After laying thirty-nine traps on the slopes of this hill,
my companions decided to throw away the last of these
             traps,
which was a pathetic, half-broken little object;
however, I went back for it, and said to my friends:
'Look, let's lay this one as well, for although it might
             look useless,
there is always the possibility that some bird may fall into it.'
Finally, we laid this trap, slightly apart from the others,
and went off to get pissed and have a good time.
Two hours later, in a rather merry state, we returned;
but fortune was not as smiling that day as we were,
and there was not a single bird in any of the thirty-nine traps.
It was then that I remembered the solitary half-broken one,
and I said: 'Let's go off to see if by some remote chance
a bird has fallen in it.' Well, we got there, and guess
what we found? Not even a feather.

FIRST GUARD: You are a very modest nobleman, Your
             Lordship;
    please go inside, today might be the lucky day
    you find the partridge falling into your trap.

CAMACHO: I am going in.
    Oh help me please, my little magic fountain,
    I carry the key to open you between my toes!
    Give me light, and wine, and some nice slices of ham,
    but don't give me any problems! That's all I ask.
    (*Exit CAMACHO.*
    Enter ESTACIO and PARIS.)

ESTACIO: Do not go in, I beg you!

PARIS: Do not hold me back; I assure you that even if the
    walls in front of me were those of Babylon,
    I would still go in.

ESTACIO: Sire, how could you possibly go in just like that
    into so dark and dangerous a labyrinth?
    What means have you of surviving?

PARIS: The very best that the human mind could have devised.
    When I tell you what I have on me,
    you shall have no more fears on my behalf.

ESTACIO: Well, tell me then.

PARIS: Do you see this sword that I am carrying?

ESTACIO: Yes, I do see the sword you are carrying.

PARIS: Take it out of its sheath.

ESTACIO: It's certainly a lovely piece of steel.

PARIS: Well, it is more than that. It's workmanship
is so intricate and ingenious that it hides a candle
inside a secret channel that extends the whole length of
the blade.
The hilt itself is hollow, and, with a slight turn of a screw,
opens to reveal all that is needed to spark a flame.

ESTACIO: This is a truly remarkable and inventive sword!
However, even though you now have light,
that is not going to last forever, and you shall
soon end up wandering lost in total darkness.

PARIS: For that reason, I have made sure to find out
the secret code that leads one to the palace.

ESTACIO: Can you reveal it to me?

PARIS: Listen, Estacio:
the architect of the labyrinth has marked
with letters a total of nine doors,
to be found on the three main streets
and on six of the ones leading off these.
Just knowing what these letters are is not enough:
you will only reach the palace if you know
what name these letters form.

ESTACIO: This is even subtler than I thought!
Tell me the letters, then.

PARIS: Two As, two Es, an X, an N, an R, a D, and an L.

ESTACIO: And if you put them all together,
what do they spell?

PARIS: Try and work it out yourself.

ESTACIO: I cannot for the life of me work out what
name begins with two As, two Es and an X.

PARIS: Of course you cannot, for there isn't any such name
However, unless you make the letters spell something,
you shall never unravel the code.

ESTACIO: Come on, just tell me!

PARIS: The letters are an anagram of Alexander.
    There is no other name that they could spell.
ESTACIO: How did you find out about the letters?
PARIS: Money helped.
    The letters are made of wood;
    and I was able to bribe the man who carved them.
    Then, when I knew what they were,
    I thought for a while, and came up with the name
    of Alexander.
ESTACIO: Your ingenuity astonishes me!
    Now you can enter the labyrinth
    free from all fear. Guards!
FIRST GUARD: Yes sir…
ESTACIO: The prince of Urbino wishes to
    risk his life in this dark contest.
SECOND GUARD: I would be grateful if Your Excellency
    stepped into this changing room
    so that you can be thoroughly searched.
PARIS: Estacio, farewell.
ESTACIO: May the fame of ancient heroes be your reward!
PARIS: I am prepared to die for Laura.
    (*Exit all. Enter ALEXANDER, lost inside the labyrinth.*)
ALEXANDER: Where now, for God's sake? where now
                                        shall I place
    these feet of mine that have been so blind and stupid
    as to trust the guidance of some mad Spaniard?
    Now I am lost thanks to his well-stocked fountain
    which I completely failed to find. Thinking that it might be
    further inside than he had said, I stepped timidly into
    the pitch black street behind, but then took a wrong turning,
    and soon lost what little sense of direction I had originally.
    After many futile attempts to get back to where I started,
    I found myself in my present situation, wandering blindly,
    guided only by a growing panic. And now, deservedly,
    my time has surely come, and my life is drawing to an end.
    Oh cunning and ingenious Florela, what a strange and
                                        complex
    way is this to avenge yourself for my deceiving you!

How much I underestimated the wiliness of your ways!
Where am I? Please, God, if you have mercy, come and
        help me!
Am I going backwards or forwards, am I near the end or
        the beginning?
Or perhaps none of this now matters, as I am bound to die.
Great God above, what path shall I take now?
(*Enter CAMACHO, also lost.*)

CAMACHO: Well, this is a right mess I've got myself into.
I suppose I saw it coming; I mean what else
could I expect for being so bloody stupid
as to go and wander inside a labyrinth.
As for that fountain, it was fucking useless.
Doubtless the Duke must have put it elsewhere,
and, silly me, I went to look for it;
but after a few paces, when I said to myself
enough is enough, I better be going back,
I realised I was walking in endless circles.
This has gone beyond a joke this has –
left without a clue as to where I am,
or without a single tiny scrap to eat.
I am going to die, and it's all my bloody fault!

ALEXANDER: I think I hear voices.

CAMACHO: Adam said it was a woman who had led him on.
But what is my excuse? All I can say is that
I was led on to my downfall by a flagon of wine.
Poor Camacho! Is this a worthy excuse for a man like me?
What sort of woman is this who has betrayed me?
A woman in the form of wine and ham!
Well, I suppose one should forgive such simple
        pleasures;
the thought of ham and wine is sometimes more exciting
than the prospect of four hundred women.

ALEXANDER: I am sure those were voices I heard.
Am I arriving at the palace?

CAMACHO: Heavens above! I might be blind,
but I haven't as yet gone deaf.
I must be nearing the palace,

because I'm convinced I
could hear people talking.

ALEXANDER: One of the voices sounds really close now;
be calm, Alexander, slow down a bit.
I do not want to lose this voice
by taking another wrong turning.

CAMACHO: Never give up hope until the very end,
that's what I've always said.
My God, if I really am reaching the palace,
think how my fortunes would change!

ALEXANDER: It must be Laura who is making these sweet
sounds.
I knew she would eventually take pity on me,
and decide that I am the only one for her.

CAMACHO: It can only be Laura whose
voice is guiding me to the palace.
Just imagine if I, Camacho,
was made today the new Duke of Ferrara!

ALEXANDER: The voice is getting even closer.

CAMACHO: Oh naked little Cupid, I'd ask you to guide
my steps
if I hadn't just remembered you were blind!
My darling Laura, is that really you?

ALEXANDER: Oh sweet light of my life,
your radiance has guided me through the darkness.
(*The two embrace.*)

CAMACHO: I'm in heaven,
I'm finally in your arms.

ALEXANDER: Who are you?

CAMACHO: I am Don Lucas. And who are you?

ALEXANDER: Alexander, you drunken idiot.

CAMACHO: Some fair Laura you are!

ALEXANDER: Camacho, it's thanks to you
that I have landed in this mess.

CAMACHO: And where do you think I've landed?
In some bed of roses?

ALEXANDER: And what happened to your fountain?

CAMACHO: If your lady love finds herself duped
and decides to have the thing removed,
what fault is it of mine?

ALEXANDER: But you've no right to complain!
You could have turned back the
moment you found the fountain missing.
Why on earth did you continue inside?

CAMACHO: To look for you, that's why.

ALEXANDER: And what can I do now?

CAMACHO: Have you got anything to eat?

ALEXANDER: Only all that wonderful food
that was waiting for me in the fountain.

CAMACHO: I should never have had anything to do with
labyrinths!
Where the hell did I leave my brain?
Hadn't I enough experience of similar dangers?
Isn't looking after a household just another labyrinth?
Or what about one of those lawsuits that go on for ever?

ALEXANDER: Oh for God's sake stop talking!
This is not the time for your home-spun philosophy!

CAMACHO: Well I've got my just deserves.
The secret of my extraordinary powers
has been taken from me for having
dared to meddle in what was not my business.
My hair has been cut off, and here I am,
condemned to die on account of a Delilah
whom I have scarcely seen let alone fancied.

ALEXANDER: I shall die before you,
you can count on that.

CAMACHO: Ssshh!

ALEXANDER: What?

CAMACHO: I hear voices.
(*Enter the INFANTE, also lost.*)

INFANTE: Look where that ball of thread has got me now!
I do not know what Theseus did with his,
but mine proved better in theory than in practice.
I had barely turned the very first corner
when the bloody thing broke,
leaving me to wander aimlessly

in a futile search to find the tail.
And now that the thread has gone forever,
what can I possibly do to find my way back?
ALEXANDER: I would say there were someone nearby.
INFANTE: Oh poor, poor me!
How am I going to get out of here?
CAMACHO: It seems a woman's voice to me.
INFANTE: Was there anyone as unlucky as me?
But…I'm sure I heard someone speak.
I must be near the palace; I'll go and see.
ALEXANDER: Camacho, this is where our ways part;
you go that way, and I'll follow the voice.
Oh Laura, my darling,
I shall soon be with you!
INFANTE: My sweet, sweet little angel,
light of my life!
ALEXANDER: You can't imagine my darling
all that I have suffered in searching for you!
CAMACHO: I am coming with you to the palace,
you can't have everything for yourself!
INFANTE: What is this? Are you a man?
ALEXANDER: Yes, and I suspect you are one too.
INFANTE: I am a man, yes.
ALEXANDER: What man?
INFANTE: The Infante.
CAMACHO: Well, isn't this cosy?
ALEXANDER: I am Alexander.
CAMACHO: And I'm Camacho, lover extraordinaire.
ALEXANDER: Where are you going?
INFANTE: I'm lost.
ALEXANDER: We're all going to die here!
INFANTE: You mean, you cannot find the way out either?
ALEXANDER: Our only hope is to start shouting.
INFANTE: I am all for that too.
Let's concede defeat,
and hope that someone hears us,
and comes to our rescue.

CAMACHO: Hello, you out there!
　　Can you tell us the way
　　to the lost persons' inn?
ALEXANDER: Laura, Laura, I give in,
　　come and look for me!
INFANTE: Laura, I am lost as well;
　　come and look for me,
　　I am waiting for you!
CAMACHO: Laura, bring back to life these lost souls!
ALEXANDER: Oh Laura, come for the two of us!
CAMACHO: And for Camacho too!
INFANTE: Laura!
ALEXANDER: Laura!
CAMACHO: Laura!
ALEXANDER: Laura!
　　(*Exit all.*
　　Enter the DUKE, FLORELA, LIRANO and FINEA.)
DUKE: Is it possible that no-one can find the palace?
LAURA: What a test of ingenuity this has proved!
FLORELA: The greatness of the reward
　　might encourage at least one
　　person to persevere up to the end.
DUKE: I pray to God, Laura, that one of the three
　　men succeeds, and proves worthy of your love.
FLORELA: If only you knew, Laura, how frightened I am
　　　　　　　　　　　　　　　　　　　　　to lose you.
LAURA: Do not worry, Felix, I shall find a way
　　of putting off any victor.
　　Our love for each other will never be broken,
　　you can be sure of that.
LIRANO: I hear footsteps and voices.
　　(*Enter PARIS, holding a small lamp.*)
PARIS: I am here. I have crossed the dark ocean,
　　and am now at the gates of my beloved's castle.
　　Farewell my little lamp, I need you no longer
　　now that I am in a world where stars are shining.
　　But why do you all look so incredulous?
　　Do you not know who I am? I am Paris of Urbino,
　　and have become today nobler even than Paris of Troy.

DUKE: This is an extraordinary surprise!

LAURA: Who gave you light?

PARIS: Your radiant features.

LAURA: But were you not searched at the entrance?

PARIS: From top to toe, and even down to the lines of my hand;
    but no-one thought of looking inside my sword,
    which has a hollow handle, and a hidden candle.
    Thus equipped I was able to follow the secret letters,
    which I found beforehand spelt the name of Alexander.
    I have come now to claim Laura as my lawful wife.

LAURA: Wait a moment.

PARIS: I shall.
    (*The shouts of ALEXANDER, the INFANTE, and*
    CAMACHO are heard offstage.)

FLORELA: What fearful sounds!

ALEXANDER: Oh, Laura!

INFANTE: Laura!

CAMACHO: Where are you, my beautiful minotaur?

DUKE: There are people lost outside;
    Go Lirano, and you, Finea,
    and bring them light.
    Now that the contest is over,
    we can help them through the labyrinth.

LIRANO: To judge from their voices,
    they must be close at hand.
    (*Exit ALEXANDER, the INFANTE, and CAMACHO.*)

ALEXANDER: I must confess I thought my days were over.

INFANTE: I have to say the same myself.

PARIS: Well I must tell you, dear sirs,
    that you have lost, for I got here first.

ALEXANDER: Paris, do not worry,
    I concede defeat.

INFANTE: We have to respect the rules of the contest.

DUKE: In that case noble sirs,
    let me give Laura's hand to Paris.

ALEXANDER: And let Paris and Laura
    enjoy a thousand years of happiness.

PARIS: Give me your hand, Laura,
    today I think I truly deserve it.

LAURA: Paris, stop there.

PARIS: What ever for?

LAURA: I am already married.

PARIS: Married?

CAMACHO: Can't anything be simple in this world?
I thought the labyrinth was over!

DUKE: What are you saying?
By heaven, if you do not give your hand this moment...

LAURA: Stop, please.

DUKE: Give it now.

LAURA: But, sire, how can this be?
Can you not see I have a husband?

DUKE: And where is he?

LAURA: Here.

PARIS: Which one among you is this vile person?
If I do not find out...

ALEXANDER: Do not look at me, Paris.

CAMACHO: Stop waving your sword, Paris,
the Marquis Don Lucas is in no mood for
parrying with you.

PARIS: I consider that anyone who has married Laura is a
traitor.

ALEXANDER: I, for one, am no such person.

INFANTE: Well if you are not, I am even less of one.

PARIS: Then, it must be this Spaniard here!
You treacherous...

CAMACHO: Calm down, please.
If it really is me that Laura loves,
then it is because of my irresistible charm,
and not because I have done anything bad,
or anything good for that matter.
Let us shake hands, Your Lordship.

PARIS: I would rather kill one hundred Spaniards
before doing so.

CAMACHO: Before we go any further,
I should explain that I am a Marquis only by proxy.

PARIS: What do you mean by proxy?

CAMACHO: I mean that my title is just
a temporary arrangement
worked out between myself and Alexander.

DUKE: Tell us, Diana,
   who your husband is.
LAURA: My secretary.
DUKE: Good heavens above!
LAURA: Diana, sir, is a man,
   and endowed besides
   with considerable manly virtues.
DUKE: Are you really a man, Diana?
FLORELA: I...
DUKE: Why are you hesitating.
CAMACHO: This is some fine kettle of fish!
   Come on you macho mistress,
   let us in on your secret
   before we all go madder than we already are.
ALEXANDER: Poor deceived Laura,
   the time has now come for me to tell you the truth:
   afterwards you can give your hand to Paris,
   for Diana is my betrothed,
   and all these games we have been playing
   have merely been her way to stop my marrying you.
   Her real name is Florela of Mantua.
LAURA: Felix, what do you have to say to this?
FLORELA: From this moment I am no longer Felix or Diana,
   and I shall go back to being just Florela.
   Forgive me, Laura, it is love, stirred up by jealousy
   that has led me to devise a labyrinth of deceits
   such as only finds in far-fetched plays.
   I have tricked you all so as to win Alexander;
   all I ask of you now is to be witnesses to our marriage.
LAURA: Paris, please forgive me too.
   I now believe that when it comes to ingenuity and deceit,
   a woman is worth a thousand of the cleverest of men.
CAMACHO: I've finally got it, the riddle I mean.
   The answer is you, isn't it Florela?
FLORELA: I do not deny that I was the person, who,
   as the riddle said, is and yet is not,
   and who loves the person whom she does not love.
   I was Felix, and yet was not Felix;

and, as for the rest, well I won't bother to explain,
we have had enough puzzles for one day.
CAMACHO: So can I infer that you now really will be
marrying Alexander,
and will not be having any other opportune changes of sex?
FLORELA: Marquis, there is nothing for it now but for us
to marry.
As for you, I am sure the Duke will be happy to give you
Finea.

DUKE: It will be the greatest of pleasures.
CAMACHO: That's not a bad exchange!
DUKE: Finea, give the Marquis your hand.
CAMACHO: And now that your hand is in mine,
and you are going to be my wife,
let me warn you again that my marquisate
is no more substantial than a ring,
and that it was Alexander, with a single sneeze,
who made me a marquis of the wind.
FINEA: I do not mind, I like you all the same.
CAMACHO: Let's hope you do so for many years to come,
for you'll have plenty of time afterwards
to be driven up the wall by all my faults.
Loud snoring, the same old boring stories,
endless dreary evenings spent staring at the fire –
for that is really what awaits us all
at the end of the labyrinth that we call desire.

The End.